LEX MUSKETEERS VOLUME II

AMARDEEP SINGH CHANDOK

Made with ♥ on the Notion Press Platform
www.notionpress.com

Contents

Contents

Disclaimer

Neither the Lex Musketeers, consisting of the articles of the different authors including images (if any) nor its editors, publishers, owners or anyone else involved in creating, producing or delivering the book or material contained therein, assumes any responsibility for the accuracy, usefulness or correctness etc of the views of the different writers. The role of lex musketeers is only up to providing a platform to the different writers for development of the habit of writing and reading.

The opinions, discussions, views are the independent thoughts of the writers and the editor or the owner makes no warranty, express or implied, with respect the material contained therein. The owner or the editors will not be liable for any direct, indirect, consequential, special, exemplary or other damages arising therefrom.

Lex Musketeers

Lex Musketeers is a project of Book Adopters Foundation, this foundation is a non profit organization, working for the welfare of the society. Prime motive of the organization is to develop the habit of reading and writing. The term 'lex' refers to the system or the body of laws and the term 'musketeers' refers to a soldier armed with a musket. The collective meaning of the term "Lex Musketeers" refers to a soldier having the arm of law.

The prime objective of the book is to provide a platform to all the persons, who are interested in writing with specific reference to law but not limited to laws only. This book is an Endeavour to cover all the norms of the nature, society and commands of the sovereign in general through the words of the different ideologies and experts of the different fields. Apart from that Lex musketeers also provide an opportunity to the layman to express his feelings and experiences towards the social aspects of the norms with aim to provide a reference to the researchers.

Book Adopters Foundation

This foundation is one of its own kind of organization, with unique aim to spread the education and to re-develop the habit of reading books with its motto that "Proper Utilization of a Book is our Paramount Consideration." This foundation is started by six intellectual personalities under the vision of Advocate Amardeep Singh Chandok, with five other persons namely Advocate Harsh Jindia, Advocate Manjeet Singh, Advocate Hiten Gupta, Advocate Hemant Sharma and Mr. Tarun Sharma. This organization is growing since its inception and successfully got various donors of the books and a thousand of readers in the locality. After its inception the foundation has spread its arena of work & apart from prime motive of the foundation for spread of education the foundation is also providing job updates to the aspirants, Filing RTI applications at nominal fees, career guidance for students and the blood donation activities under the team Management of Advocate Shubkarman Kumar, Advocate Gagandeep Kaur, Advocate Priyanka Bansal, Advocate Manju Kumari, Advocate Zinnia, Advocate Alisha Gupta, Advocate Heema, Advocate Mehak Dalla & Advocate Munish K. Bhatia,. Blood donation activities are successfully running under the Management of Hardeep Singh, Jasbir Singh (ZLA, Food & Drugs Administration Punjab) & Jaspreet Singh Kaka Machiwara.

CHAPTER I

CRIMINAL JUSTICE SYSTEM: ANTIQUARIAN PAST {Author: Arpandeep Kaur}

We know that the concept of crime has been changing with the change in the socio-economic background of society. It always depends upon the force vigour and movement of public opinion and social sanctions in the same country from time to time.[1] The extent of crime apparently varies among societies and communities and over for a given society or community.[2] The definition of both crime and the criminal justice system are the subject matter of the criminology. During the early ages, crimes were very few because of the society. With the passage of time the society has become very complex and so is in the nature of crime.

The concept of crime is essentially concerned with the conduct of the individuals in society. Crime is an act of individual associated with anti- social elements that for some reasons or the other deviate from the normal behavior pattern of individuals. Since, man's interest is the best protected in the social life of society. Therefore, every member of society owes certain duties towards the other members and also has certain rights and privileges, which he insures for him from others. It is the obligation on the state to maintain normalcy in society through crime machineries.[3]

The criminal justice system is a set of legal and social institution. It enforces the law in accordance with the defined set of procedural rules and limitations. The criminal justice system includes various major subsystems. There are the composition of one or more public institution and their staffs i.e. police and law enforcement agencies and probation agencies, custodial agencies and the most important investigating agencies. In addition, there are a number of administrative agencies their work also includes criminal law enforcement.

GROWTH OF CRIMINAL JUSTICE SYSTEM: - In India like every civilized society a criminal justice system was evolved. Its evolution was influenced by social, political, economic condition. These conditions were prevailed during different phase of Indian history. Therefore, the object of criminal justice and methods of its administration changed from time to time.

In the earlier society, there was no state or authority. The retaliatory and revengeful methods were prevailing at that time[4]. During this period the victim had himself punish the offender. Even in the advanced rig Vedic period there was mention that punishment of thief rested with the very person wronged.[5] Gradually, the individual revenge disappeared and the group revenge evolved. It arises as the man could not have grown and survived in complete isolation. Therefore his survival and existence it is necessary to live in a group. Group life necessitated consensus on ideals and the formulation of rules of behavior to be followed by its members. These rules defined the appropriate behavior and the action that was to be taken when the members did not obey the rules.[6] This code of conduct which governed the affairs of the people came to be known as Dharma.

There was great importance was given to Dharma in the early period. Everyone was working according to Dharma. There was not any necessity of any authority which compels to obey the law. The society was free from the evils.

There was never kingdom, nor the king:
Neither the punishment nor the guilty was to be punished.
People were acting according to the Dharma
thereby protecting one another.[7]

Hence the ideal stateless society did not last long. While the utility of Dharma, belief in god and god fearing attitude of people dominate the society. This gradually declines the actual affairs of society.

A situation arose when some person began to exploit the others. The stronger section exploits the weaker section of society for their selfish ends. Therefore, this situation forced the law abiding people to search for a remedy. As consequences, there was the establishment of the institution of the king and his authority over the society.

Later the institution of the king and the establishment of his authority came to be known as the state.[8] The purpose of establishing the state and the authority of the king was the protection of person and property of the people. After that king organized a system to enforce the law and to punish those who violated it. This system came to be known as the criminal justice system.

The criminal justice system traces its origin during the Vedic period, when well define law had come into existence. The evolution of the criminal justice system in the history of India is covered from Vedic period onwards and it is divided into three periods.[9]

- Hindu period
- Muslim period
- British period

HINDU PERIOD: During 1000 B.C. to A.D 1000 the criminal justice system was originated. This origin has an antiquarian past. This system was originated a way back during the ancient period of Hindus. This period of Indian history was known as the Hindu period because of the prevalence and dominance of Hindu law. The concept of crime and the criminal justice system of India owes its origin to the epics and other authoritative sources such as Naya, Mimamsha Manusmiriti and Kautilya's Arthshastra.[10] These sources clearly show that a well defined criminal policy existed in the early day of Hindu society.[11] The incidents in the Mahabharata throw light on the concept of criminal law in prehistoric Hindu society. The incident tells of two Rishis (seers) i.e. Shankh and Likhit. One of them on his way to others ashram saw some tempting fruits in the latter orchard. He took some without the permission of the owner. When he met with the owner confessed what he did and asked to owner for punishment. The culprit in this period in spite of showing intention to excuse insisted on being punished. However, he was directed to appear before the king. The king first offered to pardon him because of his being honest. The king asked to culprit to compensate the owner from the royal treasury. But the culprit insisted for punishment. Finally, the king imposed the prescribed penalty of serving the right hand of the culprit.[12] This incident illustrates that an offence could neither be compounded nor be pardoned.

The early period of Hindus enumerated the concept of Dharamraj who is the deity appointed to administer justice. The Smritis recorded the precepts for the administration of justice. The administration of the criminal justice system according to Hindu system was evidently actuated by a high sense of duty as elaborated in Dharamsutras, Dharamsastras and Arthshatras of Kautilya.[13]

MUSLIM PERIOD: The criminal justice system in the Muslim period developed from A.D1206- 1757. The Hindu rule came towards the end of the 11th century. They were attacked and defeated by foreign invaders. These foreign invaders were of Turkish race.[14] Therefore the old kingdoms gradually begin to disintegrate. There was not any development of the political institution because of never ending dynastic wars and revolution. There was not any establishment of free town and also the republics were not formed. The Indian administration was weak due to the powers and ambitions of feudal families, which became a threat to the stability of central government.

The Mohammad Ghazani was invaded India during A.D1000 -1026. He had revealed that India was vulnerable and fabulously rich country. After the Mohammad Ghazni success the Mohammad Gori attacked India. Therefore, in the year of 1192 the Mohammad Gori defeated the Prithvi Raj. Prithvi raj was a Rajput king and after defeating him the Gori occupied the Delhi. In 1206 the Mohammad Gori died. He left the Indian campaign in the hands of his slaves Qutub-ud-di-Aibak. He became the first Muslim king to rule from

Delhi. He established the slave dynasty. Subsequently the following rule the India as sultans of Delhi sultanate[15]

- Khiljis (A.D 1290- 1320)
- Tughluqs (A.D 1320-1414)
- Syed (A.D 1414-1450)
- Lodhis (A.D1415-1526)

In A.D 1526 the Babar defeated Ibrahim Lodhi. He was defeated the Babar in the first battle of Panipat. After that the Mughal Empire was established. The emperors of Mughal Empire ruled India effectively up to A.D 1707. But except the period in between A.D 1540-55. This period was ruled by Sher Shah Suri. The Muhgal Empire started declining after the death of Aurangjab in 1707. The last Muslim ruler of this empire was Bhadurshah. In India the Muslim rule came to an end in 1858. The British took over the control of Indian affairs from the East India Company.[16]

The importance of the administration of the criminal justice was emphasized by the Muslim rulers. They introduced the reforms to improve the criminal justice system. The Qutub-ud-din-Aibak was for the first time appointed as the chief justice. The system of espionage was introduced by the Balban to find the truth about the criminals. The several reforms in the criminal justice system were also introduced by the Sikander Lodhi.[17]

BRITISH PERIOD: the Criminal Justice System was established by the muslim rulers which was then adopted by the administrators of the East India Company. The queen of England granted a charter to the East India Company of London on 31st December 1600. The charter was granted for the period of fifteen years.[18] It was granted to trade into and from the East Indies and also in the country parts of Asia and Africa. The authority which was given to the East India Company enables to punish its servant for grosser offence. In 1601 the first royal commission was secured by the company. After that the company authorized to continue its privileges in perpetuity. The additional powers were also given to company for enforcing the martial law.[19]

In 1612 the company was settled in Surat. After settling, the company approached the Mughal emperor Jahangir through the Ambassador of England's King Sir Thomas roe for securing a royal order called Farman. However, in 1618 he was succeeded in securing a royal order called Farman. The Farman included following:

- To live according to their religion and law without any interference.
- To settle disputes as amongst the Englishmen.
- To have disputes as between Englishmen and local person.
- The dispute settled through local authorities.

Subsequently, the activities of the company increased, the King Charles issued a new charter in April 1616. Under this charter the company was authorized to try both civil and criminal cases. These cases were related to all people whether servants and heads of company. By this charter the England laws were for the first time applicable in the territory of India.

With the passage of time from British crown the company continued securing more and more powers and privileges. The company went on expanding its spheres not only in the business field but also in the political arena. The first landmark success in the history of the political company in India was the Battle of Plassey. Therefore, the political power of the company was established by the success in the battle of buxar of 1764.[20]

Thereafter the company continued to expand its rule till 1875. The revolt of 1875 proved fatal for a political career in India. Consequently, the East India Company was deprived by the government of India act 1858. On 1 November 1858, the proclamation of Queen Victoria of England outlined the principles on which crown would govern India.[21]

British rule in India continued till 1947. In order to control the vast area and population of India, the British had reformed the existing criminal justice system of India. They modified the existing laws, passed new laws and introduced new principles. The criminal justice system as it exists today was mostly evolved during the British period.

DEFECTS IN CRIMINAL JUSTICE SYSTEM:-

The Indian Criminal justice system faces many problems in its development. The Judicial system suffers from discrimination from certain section of society, old fashioned and insufficient institution, lack of human and technical resources, lack of investigation expertise and lack of primitive action against abuser of human rights and a level of corruption. The following are a few obstacles suffered by criminal Justice system.

1. Lack of resources

Lack of resources has been a very serious problem of Indian criminal Justice system. The Indian criminal Justice system suffers from serious under funding and understaffing and is also very slow. The population judge, ratio is very low. There is a need for training of all judicial and investigation investigating person. Corruption exists in the roots of our criminal Justice system. This contributes to spreading of torture practice to more discrimination and to miscarriage of Justice.

2. Accused oriented system

Another malafied of our existing criminal Justice system is that our criminal Justice system is accused oriented system. It means that the victim has to prove that his rights have been invaded. Accused is supposed to be an innocent, until and unless the victim proves that accused has infringed his right. In fact the victim is treated very badly in our system. He runs from pillar to post for years to prove his case. He has no role to play in the investigation.

3. Police forces are poorly equipped

Police forces are poorly trained on investigation method and also on the absolute prohibition of torture of cruel inhuman treatment. Most cases of torture by state official occur in police custody. Torture is used systematically in criminal Justice system as a method of investigation. Does the distrust of population of criminal Justice system has shown a rapid growth. In fact torture has become acceptable under extreme circumstances and for hardened criminal. The Supreme Court and High Courts of India as well as the National Human Rights Commission have handed down many recommendations to prevent torture but it has not led to eradication of torture.

4. Careless investigation

A careless investigation is another challenge for criminal Justice system. The investigations conducted are often time consuming, frustrating and very often counterproductive. The investigator often tried to construct an incident which deliberately aims to miss guide the council. It is very common and normal practice in the India judicial system, which often leads to wrong judgment, thus frustrating the victims. The investigating machinery regarding crime is terribly underdeveloped, both in terms of attitude as well as facilities.

5. Problem of discrimination

One of the major problems which serves as a severe obstacle for development of India's criminal Justice system is the problem of discrimination. It is the very seed for the systemization of torture and act as an impediment to the functioning of criminal justice system. Discrimination is based on many basis such as gender, religion, caste, authenticity and social economic and political background.

CONCULSION: The criminal justice system of India had evolved over a period of three hundred years. Initially law of Dharma as propounded in Vedas was considered supreme in Hindu period. But gradually the situation changed the king started making laws keeping in view custom and usages. During this period the administration of criminal justice system proved to be defective and confusing. After that the Muslim period in India enlightened the monarchs like Sher Shah Suri and Akbar who show great zeal to administer justice impartially. But this period also suffered from defects. The British were assuming power in India. They introduced the reforms wherever necessary. They adopted new principles modifying the existing laws wherever required and made new laws where they felt it was must. However, the institution of police, magistracy, judiciary and jails developed during the British period still continue without significant change in their structure and functioning.

The Criminal Justice System of India suffered with many problems and is in need of serious reform. Fair and effective administration of justice is the corner stone of a free society and this builds up the essential component of public confidence in the institution of government. The Criminal Justice System should give particular attention to improving the investigation, prosecution and punishment of state officials who commit crime and human rights violations. There must be prompt, effective, impartial and independent investigation into all allegations of death or disappearance or other serious human rights violations.

[1] N.K. Dutta, origin and development of Crimial Justice System in India, Deep and Deep publication, New Delhi,1900, p12

[2] Johnson, H, Elmer, "crime, correction and society," Hougthon Miffin Company,Edition 4th, London,1987,P.7

[3] Krishana Deo Gaur, Criminal law and Criminology, , Deep and Deep publication, Pvt. Ltd.2002,P-8

[4] Dr. Mriynmaya Chaoudhari, Languishing for Justice, Mittal Publication, Delhi 1995, p-4

[5] Keith.A. Berriedale, The Age of Rig Veda, The Cambridge history of India, Vol.1, Standford Priting Press,P-87

[6] Alfred Russel, The Story of Civilization.

[7] M. Rama jois "Legal and constitutional history".

[8] V.C Sarkar, Epochs in Hindu Legal History, Hoshiarpur Book Agency, Hoshiarpur, 1958,p-102

[9] The gazetteer of India vol. 2

[10] Dr. S. Suparkar, "Law of procedure and justice in ancient India, Cosmo Publication, New Delhi, 1981, p-12

[11] Prasanta Kumar Sen, Penology old and new law, Tagore Law Lecture, Abhinav publication,1929,p-20

[12] T.S Batra, " Criminal law in India, Mittal Publication, Delhi,1984, P-4

[13] DR. R.B. Pal, The History of Hindu law, Deep and Deep Publication, 1996, p-278

[14] Shah Giri Raj, Indian Police, A Reprosepect, Cosmo Publication New Delhi, 1981,p-41

[15] Dalbir Bharti, The Constitution and Criminal Justice administration, A.P.H, Publishing New Delhi, 2002 p-22

[16] Dr. Singh, " Evolution of criminal justice " Indian journal of public administration,

[17] Ibid.

[18] M.P,Jain, Outlines of Indian Legal History, Wadhava and Company, Nagpur, 1997, p-5

[19] N.V. Paranjape, Indian Legal and Constitutional History, Central Law Publication, Allahabad, 2004,p-123

[20] J.K Mittal, Indian Legal History, Central Law Agency, New Delhi, 1985, p-11

[21] Keith. A. Berriedale, "The language of the Rig-Veda", in the history of india.

CHAPTER II

RIGHT AGAINST SELF-INCRIMINATION IN INDIA {Author: Amardeep Singh} {Co-Author: Mehak Dalla}

The right against self-incrimination has its earliest manifestation in the Latin maxim '*Nemo tenetur seipsum accusare*' which means that '*No man is obliged to accuse himself*[1]. The Black Law Dictionary defines "Self-Incrimination" as a statement made or an action taken during an investigation where a suspect or witness incriminates them either explicitly or implicitly. Incriminatory responses are those that reasonably tend to firmly suggest the guilt of the accused. The right against self-incrimination was created in the middle of the 17th century as a safeguard against the brutal religious persecutions based solely on hearsay. The Star Chamber and the Court of High Commission in England drew criticism for using physical and psychological torture in addition to imprisonment as a form of punishment for suspects' refusal to speak up and as a way to get them to confess to crimes such as hearsay and other crimes against the church and the state. Ex officio oaths were used to force confessions from suspects; they had to swear before God that they would answer all inquiries honestly. Thus, a suspect who was being interrogated essentially had three options: speaking up and risking bodily punishments like torture or imprisonment; taking the oath and implicating himself; and committing perjury, which was a mortal sin. In one instance, John Lilbume, was accused of smuggling seditious books into England in 1637 and was brought before the Star Chamber on three different occasions. He argued that the Star Chamber's interrogation methods were unlawful each time he showed up and declined to take the pledge and implicate himself. The Star Chamber responded by whipping him and putting him in the pillory, fining him 500 pounds, and imprisoning him for all time. His case led to a strong public backlash against torture used during interrogations, which led to the elimination of the Court of High Commission and Star Chamber in 1641 and the subsequent inclusion of the self-incrimination provision in the Bill of Rights[2].

The Universal Declaration of Human Rights includes some elements of the right to remain silent[3]. Article 11.1 of the UDHR guarantees the right of everyone accused of a crime to a presumption of innocence until proven guilty. Art. 14(3) (g) of The International Covenant on Civil and Political Rights, 1966 to which India is a party, relates to various "minimum guarantees" and states that everyone has a right "*Not to be compelled to testify against himself or to confess guilt.*" Thus, the right not to be implicated in one's own crimes has been elevated to the status of a human right.

Right Against Self Incrimination in India

The Constitution of India, in Clause (3) of Article 20 provides a right against self-incrimination i.e "*No person accused of any offence shall be compelled to be a witness against himself.*[4]" The characteristic features of this principle are-

a. That the accused is assumed to be innocent;
b. That the burden of proof rests with the prosecution; and
c. That the accused is not required to give any statement against his will.

These submissions stem from a fear that if compulsory examination of an accused is permitted, force and torture will be used against him to trap him in fatal contradictions. Thus, the privilege against self-incrimination allows for the preservation of human privacy and the application of civilised standards in the administration of criminal justice.The Indian Constitution's Article 20 was given non-derogable status under the 44th Amendment in 1978[5], meaning that the government cannot refuse to uphold this freedom even in a time of emergency.

Components of Article 20 (3) of the Constitution of India are as follows:

1. It is a right available to a person "accused of an offence"

This right against self incrimination is available to a person; according the Apex Court the protection offered by this clause extended to incorporated body, if accused of an offence as observed in the case of "***M.P. Sharma v. Satish[6]***."

Article 20(3) will be attracted only if the proceedings start with an accusation, and the person who seeks its protection was already an accused person when he compelled to make the statement. This article will have no application if the person is not an accused at the time he makes the statement but becomes an accused by the time when later statement made by him is sought to be proved.The clause does not require "formal accusation" by the issue of process by the court rather the immunity would initiate from the moment a person is named in the First Information Report.

In the case of "***Nandini satpathy v. P.L Dhani[7]***", Smt. Nandini Satpathy, was commanded to show up at the Vigilance, Police Station, for inspection in a case registered against her under the Prevention of Corruption Act. By virtue of the first information report, in which the appellant, her son and others were shown as accused persons, investigation was initiated. She was questioned throughout the course of the investigation in response to a lengthy list of written questions. However, she repudiated, claiming protection under Article 20(3). In this case, the court examined the question as to whether Art.20 (3) applies only to a person accused or to a 'suspect' as well, who is not formally an accused, when the police is holding an investigation against him. The court observed that, the protection ought to extend to police investigations, since the enquiries under criminal statutes with quasi-criminal investigations are of an accusatory nature and are sure to end in prosecution when the offence is grave and the evidence gathered well. To deny the protection of a constitutional shield designed to defend a suspect because the enquiry is preliminary and may possibly not reach the Court is to erode the substance.

The protection is available to a person accused of an offence not merely with respect to the evidence to be given in the courtroom in the course of the trial but it is also available to him at the previous stage i.e. at the pre-trial stage if an accusation has been made against him which might in the normal course result in his prosecution.The Criminal Procedure Code contains similar protections such as section 161(2) of the Code of Criminal Procedure, 1973 grants a right to silence during interrogation by police and Section 313 (3) of the Code of Criminal Procedure, 1973 protects this right to silence at the trial. These sections establish a presumption of innocence over guilt, allow the right to remain silent during both the inquiry and the trial, and forbid any party or the court from making a statement regarding the quiet.

The words "accused of an offence" indicates that the protection is confined to criminal proceedings or proceedings of that nature before a court of lawor other Tribunal before whom a person may be 'accused of an 'offence' as defined in section 3(38) of the General clauses act, *i.e.,* an act punishable by the penal code or any special or local law. As a result, it would not apply to parties or witnesses in civil actions.

2. It is a protection against compulsion *"to be a witness"* against oneself

The expression *'to be a witness'* has been subject matter of Judicial decisions and has been interpreted differently till the year 1961 despite Supreme Court's decision in "***M.P. Sharma v. Satish Chandra and others*[8]**" decided by a Bench of 8 Judges. In this case, the question was as to whether the order as to search and seizure under section 94 Cr.P.C. was violative of guarantee under Article 20 (3).The court observed that the word "witness" in its natural sense is to be understood to mean a person who furnishes evidence. A person can be a witness not merely by giving oral evidence but also by producing documents or making intelligible gestures in the case of dumb witness (Section 119) or the like. The court gave a broad view of Art. 20 (3), that it covered not only oral testimony or statements in writing but also production of a thing or evidence by other modes.

In "***State of Bombay v. Kathi Kalu***[9]",a bench of 11 judges answered the question whether Art.20(3) is violated when the accused is commanded to give his specimen hand writing, or signature, or the impression of his palms and fingers. The judges examined the definition of the phrase "to be a witness." in Article 20(3). It aimed to distinguish between testimonial and physical evidence, concluding that the act of delivering testimonial evidence alone qualifies as "being a witness." It was observed that the expression *'to be a witness'* must be constrained to mean imparting knowledge in respect of relevant facts by means of oral statements or statements in writing by a person who has personal knowledge of the facts to be communicated to a court or to a person holding an enquiry or investigation on matters relevant to the subject under inquiry. It was ruled that 'personal testimony' was to depend upon volition. An accused has the option of providing the statement or declining to do so.. Self-incrimination refers to the dissemination of information based on the personal knowledge of the individual providing the information and only applies to "personal testimony," which must be given voluntarily. The judgment observed a witness to be one who gave oral or written statements which by themselves had a tendency to incriminate the accused. All other kinds of physical, biometric, forensic and material evidence were not considered a 'personal testimony' and did not invoke the right against self-incrimination. Their rationale was seen as only to lend reliability to other evidence. Consequently, hand writing samples, fingerprints, thumb-prints, foot prints or signatures, were declared as material evidence, not incriminating the accused and falling outside the scope of Article 20(3). The court could now direct an accused to produce or give his hand writing exemplar, under Section 73 of Indian Evidence Act,without invoking Article 20(3).

In "***Smt. Selvi v. State of Karnataka***[10]"the validity of narco-analysis, lie detector test and analysis of brain waves (Brain Electrical Activated Profiling (BEAP) test) was challenged. The three judge bench ruled that the compulsory administration of such tests should be banned as forcible intrusion into the mind of the accused violates Article 20(3) and also intrudes the privacy and liberty of an individual, thus violating Article 21 of the Indian Constitution.

3. It is a protection against such "Compulsion" resulting in his giving evidence against himself:

In order to bring the statement in question within the prohibition of Article 20(3), it must be demonstrated that not only did the person making the statement have the character of an accused person at the time he made the statement, and that it had a major influence on the criminality of the maker of the statement, but that he was also compelled to make the statement.

As a result, compulsion in this context denotes duress; it must be a physical objective act rather than the state of mind of the person making the statement, unless the mind has been so conditioned by some extraneous process that the making of the statement is involuntary and so extorted. The mere asking by a police officer investigating against a certain individual to do something is not compulsion within the meaning of Article 20(3). The mere fact that a suspect was in police custody when he gave a statement does not mean that he was forced to testify against himself. The accused may demonstrate that while he was being held by the police at the pertinent time, he was subjected to treatment that amounted to coercion. It will be a question of fact and in each case the court will decide after carefully analysing the information presented to it regarding the relevant facts and circumstances.

Section 26 of Indian Evidence Act also provides that, no confession made by a person in custody of the police may be used against them without having been made in the magistrate's presence. In case of "***Nadini Satpathy v. P.L. Dani*[11]**", the court advocated an expansive interpretation to the phrase "compelled testimony" that, It is not just physical threats or violence that are used to obtain evidence; psychological torture, environmental pressure, long-winded interrogation techniques, overbearing tactics, and intimidation techniques are all used. Any method of pressure, subtle or crude, mental or physical, direct or indirect, but sufficiently substantial, applied by the policeman for obtaining information from an accused strongly suggestive of guilt it becomes compelled testimony violative of Article 20 (3). In a case, where a trap is set and the accused speaks, there is no element of duress, coercion or compulsion, and he cannot claim the protection under Article 20(3). Further, Article 20 (3) is also not violated if the accused volunteers evidence against himself. Since the Article grants a privilege, the accused may waive it if he so desires.

Conclusion

In practically every criminal trial, the necessity for evidence and the right to personal autonomy are in conflict. The privilege against self-incrimination exists primarily to encourage the police and prosecution to look for the most reliable evidence that can be obtained through independent means. Instead, there would presumably be an incentive to rely only on the less reliable admissions gained during a mandatory questioning. An English writer once put it in a commentary on the issue in India that, if the police and prosecution were relieved of this constraint there would be a temptation "to sit quietly in the shade, rubbing red pepper into a poor devil's eyes, rather than wander about in the sun seeking out evidence."[49] However this clause has also drawn a lot of criticism. According to Jeremy Bentham, the privilege deprives the court of the best evidence regarding the defendant's actions in relation to the charged offence."[50] Yet, a voluntary confession that was obtained without the use of any coercion, threats, or promises is enough for a conviction under criminal law[12].A voluntary confession must be the result of a logical mind and free will. [52] However, as the experience demonstrates, the vast majority of confessions are not the product of the suspect's free will and reasoning intelligence or the use of third degree methods that are archaic and violent. Instead, the majority of confessions are the consequence of delusion, error, and deception. The test asks a judge to extrapolate minute details of a questioning after the event, typically with the police and the defendant giving dramatically divergent stories of what happened. This includes not just plainly discernible objective elements like the duration of the questioning and whether the interrogators physically restrained the suspect in any way, but also subjective traits particular to that particular suspect. The suspect's age, race, education, particular psychological strengths or weaknesses, and even details and events from the suspect's past that may have unconsciously influenced how he or she behaved in the interrogation room on the relevant night are just a few of the subjective factors that may enter into the equation. The court must then put all of these elements into a hat, mix them up in a totality of the circumstances approach, and reach in to try to find an answer to a question that can never be answered confidently. It entails making a decision between respecting the suspect's autonomy and giving up the chance to gather crucial and otherwise unattainable proof of crime.

[1]https://digitalcommons.pace.edu- accessed on February 25, 2023

[2] Mark A. Godsey , Rethinking the Involuntary Confession Rule: Toward a Workable Test for Identifying Compelled Self-Incrimination, California Law Review, Vol. 93, No. 2 (Mar., 2005),pp 495-97.

[3] Universal Declaration of Human Rights, 1948

[4] MP JAIN, "Indian Constitutional Law", 7TH ed., Lexis Nexis, Gurgaon. Pg.: 1099

[5] Sec. 40, The Constitution (Forty-fourth Amendment) Act, 1978

[6] (1954) SCR 1077

[7] (1978) 2 SCC 424

[8] A.I.R.1954 S.C. pg: 300

[9] AIR 1961 SC 1808

[10] AIR 2010 7 SCC 263.

[11] AIR 1978 SC 1025

[12] Section 24 Indian Evidence Act

CHAPTER III

DOWRY DEATHS AND ITS JUDICIAL APPROACH {Author: Dhruv Gupta}

The system of giving dowry to girls in marriage is an ancient Indian custom. It is in fact that portion of the parent's wealth which they wish to give to the daughter. This helps the girls in question and the groom to start a home of their own However, it is very sad that this custom has been vitiated in our times, and the system has become a menace, a social evil in our society .

Wedding are no longer happy events, but keep the brides, parents on tenterhooks lest the groom's family demand unreasonable gifts on the eve of the wedding. In fact, quite often, the greedy groom or his parents do demand gift in cash or kind such as a motor car, video, etc. which the girl's parents may not be able to fulfill. Then they are caught between the devil and the deep sea breaking off the wedding at the last minute brings infamy to the girl. Very often false, malicious stories are spread about her so that re - engagement and marriage becomes difficult. Often girls are driven to suicidal lengths because of the tension created by such a situation

Another technique adopted by the boy's family is not to make unreasonable demands before the wedding, but harass the girl after the wedding to induce her to request her parents to give the gifts they ask for. The girl is taunted at every step and her life is made a virtual hell until she can fulfill the unreasonable demands of her husband and in laws.

In such situation, the girl has no option but to accede to these demands and urge her parents to fulfill them. Sometimes, when girl knows that their parents cannot fulfill these demands, they are driven to commit suicide. Even worse is the situation where the in - laws join hands to burn the bride to death, so that the son can be remarried to someone who will get them more dowry. This is the lowest level of greediness, degradation and inhumanity to which a human being can sink, and it is indeed a very sad comment on the Indian Character, that there are innumerable examples of these happenings. Brides are shamelessly and fearlessly burnt to death to satisfy the greed of such people.

The important thing to be done here is to mobilize public opinion against It. Young men should refuse to take dowry. They should realize that marriage is a union of two souls. Marriage gives them their own family and incentive to fulfill their ambitions in their career. Rather, they should have enough self - respect to refuse the money or gifts which are offered by the bride's parents to 'buy' them. Similarly, girls too should refuse to marry a young boy who is greedy enough to demand anything from her parents. In fact, the slightest indication before marriage of the boy's greediness should warn her, and instead of being carried away by the sense of romance she should be worried of marrying such a boy.

Another important solution is for every girl to be professionally educated so that she has the ability to earn before she is married. If she is working before marriage it would be even better, for being financially independent would make her self-confident. It would be easy for her to refuse greedy young men. It would in other words, give her the supreme confidence to mend for herself. It would be difficult hurting a working girl who can answer them back in the same coin.

Finally, the real solution can only come if public opinion is strongly mobilized against the giving and taking of dowry. Till each individual regards it as an evil it would be difficult to root it out. Therefore, this should be done on a war footing and every government media should be used for this purpose. Till the old and young men women and even children regard it as a social evil not all the laws of the country can put an end to it.

Dowry system has eaten into the bones of our society. The birth of a daughter is no occasion of joy for the parents. A girl when becomes young is a burden on her parents. They have to face great difficulties in finding out a suitable match for their daughter. It is a problem to get her married in a rich and respectable family without a decent dowry. Daughter of poor parents however beautiful and well educated cannot be married to a rich man's son. Many girls commit suicide to save their parents from the evil of dowry.

This custom is the root cause of many other evils. Our Government has decided to root out this evil from Indian society. Laws are being made to put an end to this big evil. Youngman are also coming forward to raise their voice against this curse. People should take a pledge to fight this great evil at all costs. It is a slur on the fair name of this great country. Men should also try to wash off this dirty stigma.

Dowry System

The Hindu Society is full of a number of evils practices and bad customs such as dowry, which has become a major social evil against women. Today it is difficult to say how and why this evil custom started? Perhaps it might have originated from the parents desire to give their daughter a share of her parental property in the form of dowry. Every day we see how women have to suffer for the sake of dowry. Day in & day out we read the news of one or another young woman being burnt to death because she could not bring dowry with her. Torture of young bride's because of their failure to bring dowry is even more prevalent and they are forced to commit suicide. The result is that the parents of a girl have to make themselves paupers in order to arrange her marriage.

Really, a dowry system is an evil. It is spreading fast like Cancer. There are anti-dowry laws. The police have been instructed to take a serious view of 'Dowry - deaths'. But it is generally seen that crimes done for the sake of dowry are not punished. These cases fail in the courts of law.

So, law alone cannot help much in this respect. Social efforts are needed to end this evil. Young men should pledge that they would not accept any dowry. Anyone demanding dowry should be put to shame. He should be socially boycotted.

Government offices, education institution, business organizations, the armed forces etc. They are the victims of many evil practices of the society. One of them is the dowry system which is of cancerous type. Although legislative measures have been taken by the Central Government and the state Governments yet it persists in our society, eating away the very tissues of social life like a cancer.

When a female child is born in a Hindu family, particularly in Northern India, the faces of al l the members of family become sad. The very expression of joy disappears from their faces. It looks as if they had come under the eclipse to sorrows and miseries. Even the mother who has given birth to the child looks sullen and sometimes becomes the object of taunts and ironical remark of her in-laws.

All these things are happening simply because of the dowry system which is a stigma on the fair name of the Indian society and a curse for women. The parents of the girls have to provide a substantial amount of money to the parents for marriage talks. If they do not accede to their demands, the marriage talk receives a great setback. And if they agree under the force of circumstances and fail to pay it, their daughter is taunted, humiliated and subjected to cruel treatment. As a result, she begins to feel that her life is worthless, there is no meaning in living alive and she feels obliged to commit suicide. On the contrary, if she is taunt-proof, she is burnt alive by her in-laws.

Despite the statutory measures of the government, it is continuing prominently in certain parts of the country like Rajasthan, Madhya Pradesh etc. In such a case, there is no other alternative left except to mobilize the public opinion against the system of selling boys. On a war scale, this system is to be fought by all political parties and the press. The dowry seekers are to be black - listed and publicly boycotted. The youths of today have to take a pledge not to allow them to be sold to the parents of the girl. They have to come forward and decide their own fate instead of being a puppet in the hands of their parents. The black marketeers are to be eliminated because it is they could promote such a system by offering rich dowries in the marriage of their daughters. If this is done, there is every hope of eliminating the dowry system from

India.

The evil of dowry is a great insult to womanhood. It is a symbol of male superiority and woman's degradation. Due to this evil, the birth of a daughter is looked down upon and woman becomes a burden.

Dowry deaths are deaths of married women who are murdered or driven to suicide by continuous harassment and torture by their husbands and in-laws over a dispute about their dowry, making the women's homes the most dangerous place for them to be.

Dowry death is considered one of the many categories of violence against women, alongside rape, bride burning, eve teasing, female genital mutilation and acid throwing.

SITUATION IN INDIA

Dowry deaths relate to a bride's suicide or killing committed by her husband and his family soon after the marriage because of their dissatisfaction with the dowry. It is typically the culmination of a series of prior domestic abuses by the husband's family. Most dowry deaths occur when the young woman, unable to bear the harassment and torture, commits suicide. Most of these suicides are by hanging, poisoning or by fire. Sometimes the woman is killed by being set on fire by her husband or in-laws; this is known as "bride burning", and is sometimes disguised as suicide or accident. Death by burning of Indian women has been more frequently attributed to dowry conflicts. In dowry deaths, the groom's family is the perpetrator of murder or suicide.

India has by far the highest number of dowry-related deaths in the world according to Indian National Crime Record Bureau. In 2012, 8,233 dowry death cases were reported across India. This means a bride was burned every 90 minutes, or dowry issues cause 1.4 deaths per year per 100,000 women in India.

According to a 1996 report by Indian police, every year it receives over 2,500 reports of bride-burning. The Indian National Crime Records Bureau (NCRB) reports that there were 8,331 dowry death cases registered in India in 2011. Incidents of dowry deaths during the year 2008 (8,172) have increased by 14.4 per cent over the 1998 level (7,146), while India's population grew at 17.6% over the 10-year period.The accuracy of these figures have received a great deal of scrutiny from critics who believe dowry deaths are consistently under-reported.

JUDICIAL TRENDS IN INDIA

There has been plethora of judicial pronouncement on dowry deaths cases ever since the enactment of the dowry prohibition la, but even the domestic violence act and drastic change introduced by the amending acts have not been able to contain this menace, on the contrary, it is on a constant increase. In protecting the women the Indian Judiciary has removed all the procedural shackles and has completely revolutionized Constitutional litigations. The Judiciary has encouraged widest possible coverage of the legislations by liberal interpreting the terms. The judiciary by its landmark judgments had filled up the gap created by the legislative machinery. The judiciary had extended helping hands to women. The vibrant judiciary has recently exalted the dignity of women by its golden judgments.

Criminal justice is a mirror image of the state of affairs in the society and the status of its governance. It is one of the primary functions of any civilized government. At the same time, democratic societies governed by rule of law and guaranteed human rights, it is not easy to organize crime control and administer criminal justice according to the exceptions of the people. The problems are many and varied. They become more complicated the technological developments, unstable governments and economic globalization.[1] With the rise of crimes against women being on the increase, it should have followed by that judges trying the cases would display not only a greater sense of responsibility but also be more sensitive while dealing with cases of violence against women. But this has not always happens not only in the lower courts but even some of the High Courts and unfortunately even in the Supreme Court.

In this regards observations of the Orissa High Court are very instructive, the High Court observed that:

'Courts are called upon to adjudicate the complex question whether 'in-laws' have become 'out-laws' .complex question whether 'in-laws' have and have directly or indirectly contributed to snuff out the life of a woman. Dowry deaths are result of Choir disgraceful acts. But the courts have to be careful in sifting the evidence to see whether the accusations are true or are aimed at false implication In the present day comp difficult lo gauge the mischievous mind. The courts have machinations of a to trend on very slippery grounds while dealing with such cases, because, sometimes, emotions overrun realities.[2] Analysis of some decisions delivered by the higher judiciary would reveal the active judicial efforts in dealing with cases of violence against woman. The court commented critically on 'attendency' which has developed for • roping in all relatives of the in -laws of the deceased in matters of dowry death which, if not discouraged, is likely to affect the case of the prosecution even against the real culprits. In a judgment, Supreme Court expressed 'strong reservations against the practice of the police to file charges against all the in-laws in dowry death cases on the basis of the allegations of the parents of the deceased.' The Supreme Court stated that involving other relatives ultimately weakens the case. Judicial trend has been most encouraging as the same is evident from analysing the following cases. Judiciary ha s time to time been also issuing suitable directives for such cases.

Veer Singh vs State Of U.P.[3]

Heard learned counsel for the applicant and learned A.G.A. for the State.

Submission is that the applicant is the father-in-law of the deceased. The informant has been examined as PW-I before the Trial Court wherein he has stated that the deceased was married to the son of the applicant, Sanfiv, against will of the family. There was no demand of dowry. The death of the deceased took place on account of illness. Applicant alleges false implication. He is in jail since 18.05.2019 and has no criminal history to his credit.

On the other hand learned AGA has opposed the prayer for bail but could not dispute the above submissions. Keeping in view the nature of the offence, evidence complicity of the accused, submissions of the learned counsel for the parties noted herein above, larger mandate of the Article of the Constitution of India and without expressing any opinion on the merits of the case, the Court is of the view that the applicant has made out a case for bail. The bail application is allowed. Let the applicant, Veer Singh, involved in Case Crime No 71 of 2019, under Sections 498-A, 304-B, 120-B, 201/34 IPC and 3/4 Dowry Prohibition Act, Police Station Milak, District- Rampur be released on bail on furnishing a personal bond and two sureties each in the like amount to the s satisfaction of the court concerned subject to following conditions. Further, before issuing the release order, the sureties be verified. (i) The applicant shall not tamper with the evidence or threaten the witnesses. (ii) The applicant shall file an undertaking to the effect that he shall not seek any adjournment on the dates fixed for evidence when the witnesses are present in Court. In case of default of this condition, it shall be open for the Trial Court to treat it as abuse of liberty of bail and pass orders in accordance with law. (iii) The applicant shall remain present before the Trial Court on each date Axed, either personally or as directed by the Court. In case of his absence, without sufficient cause, the Trial Court may proceed against him under Section 229-A of the Indian Penal Code. (iv) In case the applicant misuse the liberty of bail during trial and in order to secure his presence, proclamation under Section 82 Cr.P.C. is issued and the applicants fail to appear before the Court on the date fixed in such Proclamation then the Trial Court shall initiate proceedings against him in accordance with law under Section 174-A of the Indian Penal Code. (v) The applicant shall remain present in person before the Trial Court on the dales fixed for (i) opening of the case, (ii) framing of charge and (iii) recording 01 statement under Section 313 Cr.P.C. If in the opinion of the Trial Court absence of the applicant is deliberate o without sufficient cause, then it shall be open for the Trial Court to treat such default as absence of liberty of bail and proceed against him in accordance with law.

In case of breach of any of the above conditions, the complainant is free to move an application for cancellation of bail before this Court.

Mahesh Kumar Vs State of Haryana[4]

This appeal has been preferred against the judgment dated 21.01.2009 passed by the High Court of Punjab and Haryana at Chandigarh, by which the High Court has allowed the appeal of Savitri Devi, mother of the appellant and affirmed the conviction of the appellant passed by trial court on 12.12.1995 for the offence punishable under Section 304-B IPC. However, the High Court has reduced the sentence of the appellant from ten years to seven years looking to the fact that the appellant had suffered a protracted trial of more than 15 years.

The trial court held that the letters written by the deceased with oral evidence in the form of statements of Complainant PW3 - Sohan Lal and PW4- Rajbir. brother of the deceased, are sufficient to establish that deceased was continuously harassed and met with cruelty on account of dowry and as such it is a case of dowry death. The trial court had come to the conclusion that the prosecution has proved its case only against Appellant/Mahesh Kumar, husband of the deceased and Savitri Devi, mother-in-law of the deceased whereas in respect of accused Rajpal and Kamlesh, the trial court held that no specific role is assigned to them and, therefore, they were given benefit of doubt and were acquitted.

State Of Haryana vs Angoori Devi[5]

This appeal filed by the State of Haryana is against a judgment and order dated 3.5.2012 passed by a Division Bench of the High Court of Punjab and Haryana at Chandigarh allowing the appeal filed by the respondents It is true, that the victim died of burns. The death was otherwise than under normal circumstances and within 7 years of marriage. However, to attract Section 304B of the Indian Penal Code, the prosecution has to establish that soon before the death the deceased was subjected to cruelty and harassment in connection with demand for dowry. The High Court rightly found that the evidence did not show any proximate connection between the demand of dowry and the act of cruelty of harassment and or the death. The prosecution has not been able to prove that the victim was subjected to cruelty or harassment soon before her death in connection with any demand for dowry.

Under Section 304B of the Indian Penal Code, the prosecution cannot escape from discharging its burden of proving that the harassment or cruelty was related to demand for dowry soon before death. In this case, the High Court has been swayed by the fact that the evidence of the complainant, being the father of the victim, did not evince direct knowledge of demand of dowry. The judgment and order under appeal is not liable to be interfered with.

Accordingly, the appeal is dismissed.

THE CHANGING SCENARIO OF DOWRY DEATH: JUDICIAL APPROACH

To constitute cruelty, the conduct complained of should be "grave and weighty" so as to come to the conclusion that the petitioner spouse cannot be reasonably expected to live with the other spouse. It must be something more serious than "ordinary wear and tear of married life". The conduct taking into consideration the circumstances and background has to be examined to reach the conclusion whether the conduct complained of amounts to cruelty in the matrimonial law. Conduct has to be considered, as noted above, in the background of several factors such as social status of parties, their education, physical and mental conditions, customs and traditions. It is difficult to lay down a precise definition or to give exhaustive description of the circumstances, which would constitute cruelty. It must be of the type as to satisfy the conscience of the Court that the relationship between the parties had deteriorated to such extent due to the conduct of the other spouse that it would be impossible for them to live together without mental agony, torture or distress, to entitle the complaining spouse to secure divorce. Physical violence is not absolutely essential to constitute cruelty and a consistent course of conduct inflicting immeasurable mental agony and torture may well constitute cruelty within the meaning of Section 10 of the

Hindu Marriage Act. Mental cruelty may consist of verbal abuses and insults by using filthy and abusive language leading to constant disturbance of mental peace of the other Party and the sustained reprehensible conduct, studied neglect, indifference or total departure from the normal standard of conjugal kindness causing injury to mental health or deriving sadistic pleasure can also amount to mental cruelty. The respondent's act of humiliating the appellant and virtually turning him out of house also amount to cruelty. The Court dealing with the petition for divorce on the ground of cruelty has to beer in mind that the problems before it are those of human beings and the psychological changes in a spouse's conduct have to be borne in mind before disposing of the petition for divorce. However, insignificant or trifling, ouch conduct may cause pain in the mind of another. But before the conduct can be called cruelty, it must touch a certain pitch of severity. It is for the Court to weigh the gravity. It has to be seen whether the conduct was such that no reasonable person would tolerate it. It has to be considered whether the complainant should be called upon to endure as a part of normal human life. Every matrimonial conduct, which may cause annoyance to the other, may not amount to cruelty. Mere trivial irritations, quarrels between spouses, which happen in day -today married life, may also not amount to cruelty. Cruelty in matrimonial life may be of unfounded variety, which can be subtle or brutal. It may be words, gestures or by mere silence, violent or non - violent."

Some of the reasons are of cruelty upon women are:-

1. Humiliating, turning out of house and not taking care during illness

Ordinarily, mere words do not amount to cruelty, but since one of the marital obligations is sobriety and kindness, habitual use of rough language, or systematic and continued use by one spouse of vile, profane and unkind language in the presence of and towards the injured spouse, constitutes cruelty if it is causing immense mental suffering and injury to the latter's health. The mere use of profane and abusive language does not constitute cruelty, at least when used only once or at .intervals. However, cruelty may consist of remarks, statements, language or words that render the life of the spouse burdensome, even if no personal violence is inflicted or threatened. Words uttered without justifiable cause and for the purpose of inflicting pain, or words tending to wound the feelings to such a degree as to affect the spouse's health or cause grave and weighty mental suffering constitute cruelty.[6]

Further observed by Hon'ble Supreme Court of India that respondents act of humiliating the appellant and visually turning him out of house and did not take care of the appellant during his prolonged illness and never enquired about his health even when he underwent the bye-pass surgery amounts to cruelty. Unilateral decision of refusal to have intercourse for considerable period without there being any physical incapacity or valid reason may amount to cruelty.[7] In another case husband has been thrown out of the house by the wife and had been forced to live sexless life amounts to cruelty by wife.[8] In another case it has been held that the husband did not cohabit with deceased wife from very first day of marriage till her death, thereby compelling her to live a life of celibacy amounts to cruelty.[9] Wife retaining house of husband and turning him out of house without any reason is ill -treatment by wife amounts to cruelty to husband.[10]

It has been observed by Hon'ble Rajasthan High Court, while deciding an appeal against Divorce on the aground o f wife's cruelty to husband and his family and False case of cruelty and dowry demand under section 498 - A IPC. that:

The respondent husband, as AW I has narrated the events of cruelty meted out to him and his family members. According to him, he has been verbally abused by the appellant wife in front of the neighbors. His family has been humiliated by the false complaint lodged with the police and with the District Woman Development Tribunal. Moreover his wife has taken away money, jewellery and utensils from the matrimonial home and given them to her parental family. In view of the repeated acts of cruelty, he finds it impossible to live with the appellant. His testimony has father's testimony as AW 2, Shadi Ram and by the testimony of the Independent witnesses AW 3, Balu Ram and AW 4 Khairati Ram. There is no reason for this court to doubt the testimonies of the independent witnesses and of the respondent's father.

Even the learned Judge has noted that the appellant is in the habit of leveling the false charges against respondent-husband and his family members. She is also prone to change her stand. She had lodged a criminal report against the respondent and his family members. In her testimony she clearly admits that a negative final report was filed by the police. But, she does not state that she had filed a protest petition against the negative final report. Although Mr. M.K. Jain had claimed, during the course of the arguments, that the trial court in the criminal case has taken cognizance on the basis of the protest petition filed by the appellant, but the cognizance order has to been produced before this Court. Hence, we are not in a position to accept the said contention. The appellant had also refused to implement the decision of the caste Panchayat and had refused to cohabit with the respondent. Without any rhyme or reason, she has refused to fulfill her matrimonial duties. Her omission does amount to mental cruelty towards the respondent husband.

Although the appellant claimed in her testimony that she is willing to resume her cohabitation with the respondent husband, but the fact that the she is staying away from the husband for the last four years, the fact that she refused lo—resume"—tier cohabitation despite the direction of the caste Panchayat, the fact that she has false cases both before the police and before the District Women Development Tribunal clearly prove her intention not to live with the husband. Since in the present case the marriage has become a dead wood, since there is no possibility of resurrecting the marriage, it is better to dissolve the said marriage interfere with the judgment dated 30.8.05.[11]

2. Husband refused to effectuate marital obligation

Marital intercourse is just one marital right or duty. There are many other important rights and duties. The obligations of the parties to each other and society do not depend on this single duty. The other obligations include fidelity, sobriety and kindness. Sexual relations between man and woman are given a socially and legally sanctioned status only when they take place within marriage. But. this obligation is of a very personal and delicate nature depends on sentiment and feelings to such an extent that it would be an intrusion into the privacy of domestic life to stipulate that reasonable denial on the part of either party to submit to marital intercourse constitutes cruelty. Thus, such denial does not constitute cruelty even though refusal to have marital sexual relations undermines the essential structure of a marriage.

If refusal is occasional, or for a short period, it is against public policy to treat it as cruelty. However, complete failure to have sexual intercourse over a prolonged period, or its total and irrevocable negation, despite advances and requests, does constitute cruelty as in the absence of an adequate excuse, such refusal strikes at the basic obligations springing from marriage, undermining its essential structure.[12]

In recent case, it has been held that husband not capable of performing matrimonial obligations and marriage could not be consummated moreover, husband not ready for medical check - up, held, marriage without sex is an anathema and amounts to cruelty.[13]

It was observed by the Rajasthan High Court that it is established that respondent husband refused to effectuate his marital obligations. He had avoided consummation of marriage on one pretext or other; persistent refusal to consummate marital intercourse and discharge marital obligation amounts to cruelty.[14]

3. False allegation of extra marital relationship

In this case decided by Andhra Pradesh High Court held that where the husband in divorce petition had only said that he was subjected to harassment and cruelty which cannot be put on record since the kind of allegations leveled by his wife were not only harmful and derogatory to. him in society but also to family of his sister-in-law but the wife had blown up the allegations in counter and made such elaborate allegations and same unethical and unholy allegations linking up character of husband with the character of sister-in-law and thereby bringing down reputation of the family of sister-in-law of husband it only indicates the amount of abhorrence the wife gathered against her husband. Her thought process was absolutely going wrong in a short span of 11 months of marital life instead of understanding the husband or correcting the husband, if at all he was at fault and thereby make a good family by herself and for herself, the wife had resorted to demolish her own family and her future and the future of other family members of the husband. Thus the conduct on the part of wife was such that her desertion was not justified and cruelty if at all was to be attributed to wife only. Subsequently she made a complaint to Bar Council of Andhra Pradesh, Hyderabad making the same allegations targeting the husband and the sister -in-law of the husband. She can have grievance against the husband for any reason but has absolutely no right to demolish or to destroy the family fabric of the sister-in-law of the husband. She had lodged criminal proceeding against husband and in -laws under S. 498- A. IPC and said proceedings ended in acquittal. In view of above facts on the ground of cruelty the husband was held entitled to decree of divorce.[15] Further Punjab and Haryana High Court held while granting a decree of divorce on the ground of cruelty and irretrievable breakdown of marriage to the husband observed that denial of sexual intercourse by wife to husband constitute mental torture toward husband.[16]

4. Physical violence for demand of dowry

Sometimes words inflict a more painful blow but, under Section 498 - A, IPC physical harassment for the demand of dowry is a punishable offence. In a recent case, the accused husband threatened that whenever his wife comes to his house, she will not come alive to her parents. On another occasion accused slapped his wife. These two incidents are sufficient to hold accused guilty of offences under section 498 - A and 306 IPC where wife committed suicide.[17] In another case it has been observed that there had been persistent demand of colour T.V., scooter and Rs. 20,000/- deceased was subjected to harassment, humiliation and physical violence and beating by the husband and her-in-laws. Dead body was secretly and clandestinely cremated causing disappearance of evidence of offence, without even intimating the parents of the deceased who were living only a few miles away from their village. The above acts fall within the definition of cruelty under section 498 - A IPC.[18]

In Sahebrao's case,[19] it has been held that where the husband and brother of the husband of deceased were demanding Rs. 10.000. She was constantly troubled and given beating. Her father was insulted in her presence, the Act of the accused is sufficient to cause cruelty. In another case, accused husband and in-laws subjected deceased to cruelty and harassment for not bringing balance dowry amount, leading her to commit suicide is sufficient to convict the accused u/s 498 - A.[20]

In a recent case, it has been observed by the High Court that the accused husband given beating to deceased because the wife sold some agriculture product without permission of the husband and she committed suicide. The accused husband is convicted for causing cruelty and abetment of suicide.[21] In another case, the accused husband was not satisfied with the quality of articles given during marriage. The husband did not allow the deceased to meet anybody and, in fact, she was kept confined within her room. She was not given proper food and finally, there was persistent demand for a scooter by the accused to be brought from the father of the deceased wife. These all act would bring the appellant/ accused within the mischief of sec. 498- A of the IPC.[22]

In another recent case decided by Hon' ble Supreme Court, it has been held that the accused demanded Rs. 25000/- from the father of the deceased for purchasing a tempo. This demand was not fulfilled due to weak financial position of the father of deceased. The deceased was often beaten and was sometimes not given food. After the wife was murdered, information was sent to her parents that she had died on account of snake bite. The accused had been convicted for dowry death and cruelty.[23]

In another recent case decided by Hon'ble Supreme Court, it has been by the Apex Court that the deceased had been harassed due to demand of dowry. About 6 months prior to the occurrence, the appellant husband demanded Rs. 80,000/- for purchase of tractor. However, the brother of the deceased could not fulfill the demand of money. Surender, the deceased husband started beating the deceased and ultimately she was turned out of the matrimonial house and went to her parent's house. Thereafter, she was taken aback by the appellant, but 10 days after she committed suicide. Accused are convicted for cruelty and dowry death.[24]

JUDICIAL RESPONSE ON DYING DECLARATION IN CASE OF DOWRY DEATH

The Principle on which dying declaration is admitted in evidence is indicated in legal maxim " *nemo moriturus proesumitur mentiri*- a man will not meet his maker with a lie in his mouth." The expression dying declaration has not been used in any statute- It essentially means statements made by a person as to the cause of his death (sec. 32 of Evidence Act). The grounds of admission are: firstly necessity for the victim being generally the only principal eye-witness to the crime, the exclusion of the statement might deflect the ends of justice; and secondly, the sense of impending death, which creates a sanction equal to the obligation of an oath. Dying declaration is only a piece of untested evidence and must like any other evidence, satisfy the Court that what is stated therein is the unalloyed truth and that it is absolutely safe to act upon it.[25]

Recently, Hon'ble Supreme Court held that, in dowry cases, the trial court can convict the accused on the basis of the victim' s dying declaration if prosecution witnesses turn hostile. Further held that, "once the court is satisfied that the declaration was true and voluntary, undoubtedly, it can base it conviction without any further corroboration. It cannot be laid down as an absolute rule of law that dying declaration cannot form the sole basis of conviction unless it is corroborated. The rule requiring corroboration is merely a rule of prudence.[26]

Suggestions

The need of the hour is to replace hatred, greed, selfishness and anger by mutual love, trust and understanding and if women receive education become economically independent, the possibility of this pernicious social evil dying its natural death may not be a dream. As regars the implementation of the dowry prohibition laws, it is often alleged that anti Dowry legislations is observed more in breach than in implementation. There is also need to create social awareness and mobilize public opinion against dowry through an intensive education programs at all levels particularly in rural pockets. In view of the foregoing discussions and observations, the following suggestions are made to modify the relevant provisions by means of suitable amendments and by sensitizing the police, judiciary and to some extents the women and the society at large.

1. Preventing steps like Appointment of Dowry Prohibition Officer should be taken by all the State Government.
2. Speedy clearance of Dowry cases.
3. Legal help to Victims
4. Creating awareness about penal provisions.
5. Education of women to curb dowry deaths.
6. Appointing an advisor to the police department to handle women's issue
7. Establishment of reconciliation centre
8. Deterrent punishment for dowry deaths.

Conclusion

There is no denying fact that women are still the oppressed class and therefore need protective laws and procedures but what is disturbing is that some laws and procedures have a potential of misuse. Barbarity against married women in India despite stringent laws is one aspect-broadly discussed, debated, analyzed and often becoming headlines. Also, Special statutory provisions are aimed at guarding the interests of wives but unfortunately, they are double edged weapons and if misused they cause a lot of harassment to the non-complainant. In many cases a women may be a victim of dowry harassment but surely not all cases of unhappy or strained relations can be attributed to dowry demands. Women may feel harassed and frustrated for many other reasons like, lack of privacy or independence in joint family incompatibility, drinking, smoking or other habits of the husband, financial stresses, and psychopathic problems and so on. Why then Dowry be made a scapegoat for everyone unpleasant situation. There are multifarious ways in which cruelty is committed on the wives, if one made a critical survey of the cases that comes to the police station as well as women cell daily. In majority of these cases women agree to compromise with their husband as they want to patch up with erring husband for the sake of social stigma for being a deserted wife or it is for the sake of children.

[1]Madava Menon, N.R. (Ed.), Criminal Justice India Series, Vol. 3, U.P. 2001

[2] Baby V. State of Orissa, 1984, Cr.L.J., 1684 Orissa High Court

[3] AIR 2020 ALLHC 1257

[4] AIR 2019 SC 1042

[5] Air 2019 SC 1801

[6] J.D. Kapoor (J.), Law and Flaws in Marriages, Konark Publishers Pvt. Ltd., Delhi

[7] Samar Ghosh V. Jaya Ghosh, (2007) 4SCC 511

[8] Smt. Krishana Devi V. Brij Bhusan, AIR 2007 P&H 43

[9] Alok haldar Vimal V. State of Uttaranchal, 2007, Cr. L.J. (NOC) 3 (U.T.R.)

[10] Smt. Krishana Devi V. Brij Bhusan, AIR 2007 P&H 43

[11] Sumitra v. Luna Ram, 2007(2) RLW, Rajasthan High Court, (JB).

[12] J.D. Kapoor (J.), Law and Flaws in Marriages. Konark Publishers Pvt. Ltd., Delhi

[13] Vinita Saxena v. Pankaj Pandit, 2006(1) HLR 586 (S.C.).

[14] Smt. Kusum v. Omparkash, AIR 2007. Raj. 5.

[15] B. Srinivasulu v. Mrs. Veena Kumari, AIR 2008 Andhra Pradesh 20

[16] Jasminder Singh v. Mrs. Prabhjinder Kaur, AIR 2008 P&H 13

[17] Raj Kumar v. State of MP, 2006 (4) RCR (Criminal) 508 (MP) (Jabalpur Bench)

[18] Ram Badan Sharma v. State of Bihar, 2006(4) RCR (Criminal) 104 S.C.

[19] Sahebrao & others v. State of Maharastra, 2006 (2) RCR (Cri.) 855 (SC).

[20] Pathan Hussain Basha & ors. v. State of A.P., 2007 Cr. L.J., (NOC) 1 (A.P.) (DB)

[21] Shankar Rajwar and another v. State of Jharkhand. 2007, Cr. L.J. (NOC), 97 (Jhar.)

[22] Tapas Kumar Ghosh v. State of Bengal. 2007 Cr. L.J. 434.

[23] Trimukh Maroti Kirkan v. State of Maharashtra, 2007, cr. L.

[24] Surender v. State of Haryana, 2007 Cr. L.J. 779 (SC).; Mustt. Sureya Begum v. Md. Abdul Wahid and another, 2007, Cr. L.J. (NOC) 136 GAU.

[25] Shyam Shankar Kankaria vs. State of Maharastra, 2006 (4) RCR (Criminal) 239 SC

[26] Hindu, dated 24 Jan, 2008

CHAPTER IV

CHALLENGES FACED BY INDIAN JUDICIARY AND POLICE WHILE CURBING CRIMINAL MINDS {Author: Vipul R R Malhotra}

1.1 Introduction-

In all the societies from primitive to those which have reached the highest peak of civilisation- in one or other form there is a law. The differences between the laws of two societies is not only that of the stage of development but it is also in characteristics. However, the term law means and includes different things with the existence of various different societies. The corresponding word for the term law in Hindu system is Dharma, in Roman system it means Jus, in French system it is Droit, in Islamic system it is called as Hukum, in German system of existence it usually means Richt. These words convey different meanings and ideas. Any definition of law which fails to include all these meanings would not be a good definition. Prima facie, in context to study the challenges faced by judiciary and Police while curbing crime, a learner must have a knowledge of law, need of judiciary and Police etc. Judiciary is essential to maintain and protect the principles of criminal justice system which will further help to build a crime free society. It is essential to maintain a system of checks and balances to abide the functioning of other organs of the govt. of the State as per law as explained under Article 13 of the Indian constitution as well.Finally, it is essential to impart justice for criminal, civil and any other form of dispute.

Taking reference from the National police commission[1] set up by the govt. of India in 1977 the duties and responsibilities of the police includes the power to endorse and safeguard public order, investigate crimes, identify problems that lead to criminal activities.According to India Police Act of 1861[2], Police is a civil force used to investigate crime and acts as supportive element of Indian judiciary as well as of Criminal justice system as well. Though the above referred principles of criminal justice system including the functioning of Police and Judiciary are boon for the existence of a peaceful society but still there are many no. of trials and cases which are yet to be decided by Indian judicial court complexes and are pending in their existing status. This raises question mark on the working system of Police and Judiciary as well. So in order to answer this question regarding pendency of trials in India, we have a need to perform a satisfactorily research to study challenges faced by Police and Judiciary while curbing crimes and after studying those challenges we have to find solution to sort out those challenges to make Indian system of investigation more efficient.The major challenges faced by Judiciary because of disobedience of principles of criminal justice system by police includes the following-:

1. Because of disobedience or either lack of knowledge of basic principles of criminal justice system, it is foundthat many times police delay's the filling of challans in the court of law on time.
2. Furthermore, because of this reasonable instance, Police further fails to produce the accused person on time in the court of law.
3. Thereafter, it has also been found that most of the individuals belonging to the police force are not so much trained to proceed with the aspect of lawful ambits unlike professionals of law such as Lawyers, Judges, Advocates, Researcher etc.

Furthermore, the challenges faced by Police because of disobedience of principles of criminal justice system by Judiciary includes-:

1. As we have discussed earlier also that many of the Policemen are not as much trained in the field of law. Thus because of this reason they sometimes fail to understand the complex

procedure and ambits of court of law.

2. Many a times Police officials are not supported by prosecutors, Judges and anyother trainee of law, even at instances where police officials need their help as well.

Thereafter, at instances it has been found that Judiciary has to interfere in the independent investigations being conducted by Police which clearly states that somehow Police officials lack certain knowledge of law, which is the major bane for present day world as a result of which pendency of cases, in numbers, is increasing day by day.The Supreme Court has held in Bhajan Lal case[3] that the High Court can quash the FIR to protect the accused from malicious prosecution. It has quashed the criminal proceeding against the Bhajan Lal, the then Chief Minister of Haryana. When a criminal proceeding is instituted with mala-fide intention to harass the person, the court can quash the entire proceeding for the ends of justice. The Supreme Court has issued seven guidelines which should be followed by the Court in the exercise of its inherent power vested by sec. 482 Crpc[4].

1. Where the allegations made in the first information report or the complaint, even if they are taken at their face value and accepted in their entirety do not prima facie constitute any offence or make out a case against the accused.
2. Where the allegations in the first information report and other materials, if any, accompanying the FIR do not disclose a cognizable offence, justifying an investigation by police officers under Section 156(1) of the Code except under an order of a Magistrate within the purview of Section 155(2) of the Code.
3. Where the uncontroverted allegations made in the FIR or complaint and the evidence collected in support of the same do not disclose the commission of any offence and make out a case against the accused.
4. Where the allegations in the FIR do not constitute a cognizable offence but constitute only a non-cognizable offence, no

investigation is permitted by a police officer without an order of a Magistrate as contemplated under Section 155(2) of the Code[5].

5. Where the allegations made in the FIR or complaint are so absurd and inherently improbable on the basis of which no prudent person can ever reach a just conclusion that there is sufficient ground for proceeding against the accused.
6. Where there is an express legal bar engrafted in any of the provisions of the Code or the concerned Act (under which a criminal proceeding is instituted) to the institution and continuance of the proceedings and/or where there is a specific provision in the Code or the concerned Act, providing efficacious redress for the grievance of the aggrieved party.
7. Where a criminal proceeding is manifestly attended with mala fide and/or where the proceeding is maliciously instituted with an ulterior motive for wreaking vengeance on the accused and with a view to spite him due to private and personal grudge.

The High Court can quash the FIR if it does not disclose the commission of a cognisable offence. FIR relates with commission of a cognisable offence only. Officer in charge of the police station cannot record any information (FIR) pertaining to the non-cognizable offence under sec. 154 of the CrPC. Cognisable offences are serious offences. If FIR does not disclose cognisable offence, the investigation on such an FIR will impede the rights of accused. * In Ramnaresh v/s. State of Chhattisgarh (2012) it has been held by hon'ble court of law that the conviction of accused is unsustainable if the linking evidence is missing against the accused.

1.2 Statement of the Research Problem-

The present research work is triggered to tackle and answer large number of questions and debates aboiut the challenges faced by Judiciary and Police to curb criminal minds and furthermore it will study the aspect of increasing number of pendency in deciding trials in India- A fastest developing State from entire globe. The study will not only throw light on these subjects but instead it will also help to provide solutions to tackle these problems and such solutions are going to benefit the constitutional aspect of Indian territory by overcoming those challenges. The major challenges includes the following-

1. Why Indian judiciary has failed to decide a lot number of cases on reasonable amount of time?
2. Why Police fails to investigate and sometimes fails to register FIRs in criminal cases?
3. What is the impact of wrongful investigations and pendency of trials on layman?
4. How India will tackle and solve the problems to make our State, "SONE KI CHIDIYA" again?

Thus, by providing answers to above-referred questions, the study will help the layman by providing solutions to their problems, for example, if a police official refuses to register FIR in a criminal, cognizable case, then he or she has the right to approach its superior officer for the same.

1.3 **Significance & Purpose-**

The research study would attempt to develop a report leading to identifying and installation of critical criminal law as a discipline. The research would further attemptto study the drawbacks of criminal justice system and will further ensure the ways to overcome these challenges or drawbacks by providing the satisfactorily ways to modify &* to refine the functioning of the police department and by transforming the complex structure of Indian judicial system into simple one plus to train the police officers with the complex procedural aspects of Indian judiciary as well.

1.4 Literature review-

1. The Indian Penal Code, 1860 by Prof. S.N. Mishra- It gives a satisfactorily explanation to crime, criminology, criminal justice system and principles of criminal justice system anf helps to understand the basics of criminal laws in India.

2. Reformation of Indian Judicial System, by Alexander P.J.- It provides a basic idea regarding the subject of challenges faced by Indian Judicial system to tackle crime in such a large nation, that is, India, which has a large no.of population and whose geographical area is also very large.

3. Administration of Justice in India by Mann T.K.-It provides certain solutions to be undertaken to overcome all those challenges faced by judiciary which will help to reduce pendency of cases.

4. Police, Politics & Citizens rights by Malviya P.D.- The writing studies two aspects which screens Police to work in an effective manner. First aspect deals with the lack of knowledge of vast Indian laws due to which Police fail to work effectively and second aspect deals with the great involvement of Politicians during investigation conducted by Police which is a bane for Policemen and layman of India.

1.5. Research design-

The analytical plus exploratory research design were implemented in this research study. It is also the effective study to fulfil the requirements of this research study. This analytical research provides satisfactorily answers to the questions which collides with the research work. Hence, we can conclude that the above adopted method of research design is very well suited for this research work as well. The study is based on the challenges being faced by the police department because of the complex structure of Indian judiciary & the vice versa. Hence, it is a systematic approach to provide answers to the drawbacks being faced by the present working of criminal laws and its procedural aspects as well. Furthermore, this study is basically confined to the purpose of data collection on the ground that the working procedure among various principles and agencies of criminal justice system are almost similar across the Country.

The research would combine the doctrinal methods of identifying, collecting and interpreting the relevant data. The doctrinal techniques would entail the instruments like critical deduction, comparative analysis and meta-analysis on the subject. The idea is to conduct a survey with the expert respondents to generate specific data in the form of their reflections on sociological implications of principles of criminal justice system on police, judiciary and society at large.

1.6. Research Gap-

Though a researcher had studied a number of books before entailing theresearch work, but all the thinkers, philosophers, jurists, authors are focusing on meaning of crime, criminology and there are many few of them who have just focused on challenges faced by Judiciary and Police to curb crimes In India and the researcher has not found any of the writing which provides solution to curb all these challenges, but researcher in this present research study is going to focus on the principles to be followed to curb these challenges which will be a boon for upcoming learners of criminal laws and for the entire Indian State as well.

1.7 Results & Suggestions-

Though we have earlier discussed the major challenges faced by Judiciary and Police to investigate the cases and to curb criminal minds in India but it is not sufficient to study these challenges only, but instead of this, there is a need to accept these challenges and after such acceptance, there is a need to provide solutions to curb those challenges. Today, in present era of pendency of large no. of cases in India, there is a need and obligation on Judicial officers and intelligent Advocates, Academicians of Law to come in front and to introduce an era of legal aid camps and clinics for Police officers and layman to impart them the vast knowledge of Indian Laws of Justice. Furthermore, there is a need to impart knowledge of PILs, in case of infringement of any consolidated right of large group of individuals under Articles 32 and 226 of Indian Constitution as well.

1.8 Conclusive Proofs-

Hence finally it is concluded by the researcher from the above trial that, "judiciary and police are the leaves of a tree whose basic purpose is to provide the fruit of discipline to the people of society at large as well."

1.9. References-

A.

[1]National Police Commission (recommendations), 1977

[2]Bareact, Indian Police Act, 1961,Universal Law Publications, 2022.

[3]State of Haryana Vs. Bhajan Lal 1992 Supp (1) SCC 335.

[4]Bareact, The Code of Criminal Procedure, 1973, Shree Ram Law Publishers, 2023.

[5]Bareact, The Code of Criminal Procedure, Shree Ram Law Publications, 2023.

CHAPTER V

CONSTITUTIONALISM AND JUDICIAL PROCESS IN MODREN INDIA {Author: Ginni Singla} {Co Author: Dr. Gurpreet Kaur}

The Indian Constitution gives social, political, economic, and development goals a framework. It offers the commitment to India's population to assert, ensure, and accomplish national goals in a democratic and socio-equal way without resorting to violence. The liberal, welfare state, and centralised federalism concepts are the core of the constitution. Our Preamble[1], Fundamental Rights[2], and Directive Principles of State Policy[3] all embrace these ideas.

Part III of A formal declaration of basic rights is included in the Indian Constitution, which is regarded as a feature of democratic republics. The government is constrained by these liberties. Any rights guaranteed to people in Provisions Of the constitution cannot be restricted or eliminated by legislation enacted by the state. If such legislation is approved, the courts could find it to be unconstitutional, but just declaring some fundamental rights won't help if there is no system in place to make them law if necessary. As a result, our constitution grants the Supreme Courts the authority to grant Writs as effective remedies HAEBEAS CORPUS, MANDAMUS, PROHIBITION, and CERTIORARI.[4]

CONSTITUTIONALISM

Constitutionalism basically means having a small or constrained government. Constitutionalism is the opposite of arbitrary power. "Constitutionalism" acknowledges the need for a state with authority but also demands that such powers be subject to restrictions. Despotism is the opposite of constitutionalism. A government with unchecked authority may become authoritarian and tyrannical, endangering the rights of the people. A country only has "constitutionalism" when its Constitution strives to equitably distribute rather than concentrate it in one place and sets additional restrictions and constraints thereto.

THE JUDICIARY SUPPORTING THE RULE OF LAW AND CONSTITUTIONALISM

The objective is to create the law and order, and it would be accurate to argue that Indian Constitution is far better in this regard than other international constitutions. The goal is to provide citizens with certain standards of behaviour, citizenship[5], justice, and fair play in addition to security and equality of citizenship, which will aid in the process of nation-building. One component of what Dicey refers to as the rule of law in England may be the assurance of equality before the law. It means that no one is above the law and that regular courts have jurisdiction over everyone, regardless of status or circumstance. No one must get harsh, impolite, or unequal treatment, even when doing so secures the basic requirements of law and order as prescribed by the rule of law. Several international conferences have explored the idea of the rule of law. Rule of Law is excellent as a remedy for the current state of affairs because it places a strong focus on excluding government arbitrariness, lawlessness, and unreasonableness.

The Constitution has sufficient guarantees that the independence of the court and its review process would be upheld. Review is described as a "fundamental component of the Constitution by the Supreme Court in the case of Minerva Mills Ltd. v. Union of India[6]Equal protection under the law is guaranteed under Article 14 of the Constitution. Due to the application of this constitutional article to control administrative powers to prevent them from becoming arbitrary, it has now taken a significant role.

The Supreme Court has cited the Rule of Law[7] several times in its decisions to emphasise particular constitutional norms and standards. For instance, Justice BHAGWATI emphasised in Bachan Singh that unreasonableness and arbitrary behaviour are prohibited under Rule of Law. He has said that in order to achieve this, a democratic legislature is necessary, but that it shouldn't have uncontrolled power, and that there should have been an independent judiciary to defend the people against violations of executive and legislative authority.

The Chief's ability to influence tribunal justice was prohibited by a Supreme Court ruling in P. Because that "violates plainly, a fundamental and crucial element of the Constitution is the principle of law," Sambamurthy v. State of Andhra Pradesh[8]

Review is a key component of Rule of Legislation and a crucial derivative from the phrase " The state's bureaucracy and government bodies are all reviewable examination, which comprises assessing the legitimacy of the legislation and the acceptability of administrative action; as a result, they are all responsible to the courts for the legality of their activities. Review is seen as such a significant issue in India that it has been referred to as the "fundamental feature" of the Legislature, which cannot be altered even by the use of the legislative power.

The judiciary in India is led by the Supreme Court. But before anything else, it's important to comprehend the judiciary's function. But first, we must comprehend the function of the judicial system. In India, courts are in charge of handling and making decisions on a variety of matters, including how a school should treat its pupils and whether or not two states may share resources. People can be punished by the courts for the crimes they commit. The judiciary oversees virtually every social issue that requires a law, such as

- Resolution of Disputes: Whenever a conflict arises, the courts step in to offer a resolution. The court is in charge of resolving disputes, whether they be between individuals, between individuals and the government, between two state governments, or even between the federal and state governments.
- Judicial Review: The Indian Constitution is ultimately under the control of the court. As a result, the court has the authority to invalidate legislation approved by the Indian Parliament if the

fundamental principles of the constitution are violated. Judicial Review is the term for this procedure.

PREAMBLE AND JUDICIARY RESPONSIBILITY FOR ABIDING SEPARATION OF POWERS

In continuation of what I mentioned in the earlier lines, there is a very fine line separating judicial interpretation from judicial law, and doing so might easily lead to misunderstanding. It is also claimed that judicial legislation has evolved into judicial activism However, in order to employ this device to defend the preamble; the court has also taken on the responsibility of filling the legislative gap.The voids created by the Constitution's omissions and abeyances have been addressed by the expansion of norms within the parameters of the applicable laws and on the basis of the preamble.The Supreme Court of India conducted this exercise in accordance with the constitutional preamble and design.

The Indian Constitution is said to begin with those words in the Preamble, "WE THE PEOPLE OF INDIA"[9]who approved, implemented and upholds by the Indian people beginning 26th January 1950. The People "resolved to constitute India into a 'SOVERIGN, SOCIALIST, SECULAR and DEMOCRATIC REPUBLIC'[10].

The provisions of the Constitution fully embrace each of these objectives. The Constitution's Preamble is a component of it and may be found there be invoked in the same manner as any other provision for instantaneous application, in contrast to the Preamble of Acts. Therefore, any Preamble amendment that breaches the Constitution's essential principles might also give rise to judicial action. Additionally, the court endeavoured to put the principle of constitutionalism into practise in this instance, Kesavananda Bharati v. State of Kerala[11]. This is one method the judiciary protects constitutionalism, according to India's Preamble.

CONSTITUTIONALISM IS SUPPORTED BY LEGAL CHALLENGES BY THE JUDICIARY

The judiciary has the power to review legislation, executive, or even judicial actions to ensure they comply with the Constitution. Judicial review is the method through which the judiciary keeps tabs on how the other government coordinating organizations exercise their jurisdiction. It has the power to look into whether a bit of legislation and any behaviour is legal. The rule of law and theconcept of the separation of powers are the cornerstones of judicial review doctrine. The separation of powers is tested and balanced by judicial review.

The main goals of Judicial Review are as follows:

- To ascertain if legislative acts are unlawful.
- To uphold the supremacy of constitutional law.
- To safeguard fundamental rights.
- To preserve federal balance between the federal government and the states.
- To prevent arbitrariness, unreasonable harassment, and unconstitutional legislation.

In India, the judiciary has the authority to provide a check and balance between the legislative and executive branches.The Indian Constitution has a number of clauses that expressly provide the courts the authority to conduct judicial reviews, including Articles 13, 32, 131–136, 141–143, 226, 227, 245, 246 and 372.

The Supreme Court of India has ruled that the power of the Supreme Court and High Court is an essential component of the constitution and cannot be altered by a constitutional amendment. During the judicial examination, any legislative act or executive order of the federal or state governments that is found to violate the Constitution will be ruled unconstitutional.

The statute specifically mentions the Supreme Court and High Court's ability to conduct judicial reviews in Article 13 of the Indian Constitution. In the historic case of A.K.Gopalan v. State of Madras[12]

IMPORTANT RULINGS ON THE APPLICATION OF CONSTITUTIONALISM INCLUDE

After the A.K. Gopalan case in the following instance of L. Chandra v. Union of India[13]the court provided the Judicial Review particular parameters and stated that it is important to make sure the legislation is compatible with the constitution when it is being interpreted. The significance of coherence is demonstrated in this situation.

In the matter by Shankari Prasad v. Union of India[14] it was contended that the alteration should not be recognised as valid since it breaches Part-III of the Indian Constitution. The Supreme Court stated that any component of the constitution, along with the basic rights, may be changed under Article 368, which provides the legislative body the ability. The court here applied its judicial review power.

Similar to this, When deciding whether the 17th Amendment Act of 1964 was legal in Sajjan Singh v. State of Rajasthan[15], the court followed the guidelines established in the case of Shankari Prasad v. Union of India, which established that the parliament has the power to amend the constitution under article 368.

In Bandhua Mukti Morcha[16], the Supreme Court declared that the right to life guaranteed by Article 21 also included the right to live with dignity and without being exploited. As part of a continuing legal process, the courts have so been intervening judicially in situations involving violations of human rights.

The Preamble of the Indian Constitution, which upholds the values of justice, liberty, and equality[17], has endorsed the Rule of Law[18]. All other legislation must now comply with the Constitution, which has been declared the nation's guiding document. However, it is up to the courts to declare any statute unconstitutional if it is determined to be in violation of any Constitutional clause.

THE JUDICIARY'S CHECKS AND BALANCES ARE USED TO SAFEGUARD

CONSTITUTIONALISM

Although it is no longer possible to have a tight division of powers as it was in the classical sense, the theory behind this idea is still sound. This doctrine's reasoning relies more on polarity than it does rigid categorization, which means that the centre of power needs to be diffused to prevent absolutism. As a result, the theory is best understood as a system of checks and balances.

The Supreme Court repeatedly declared in the early years that there were no limitations on the modifying powers of Parliament in Sankari Prasad (1951) and Sajjan Singh (1965). Because of this, the First Amendment (1951), Fourth Amendment (1954), and Forty-second Amendment (1976) were all attempts by governments to bypass the original Constitution. Only in the 1973 Kesavananda decision did the court start enforcing the fundamental structure concept and restricting governmental authority.

CHALLENGES THE COURT MUST OVERCOME TO SUSTAIN CONSTITUTIONALISM INCLUDE

For judgments involving the liberties, obligations andjudges have the last say over the rights and obligations of natural and legal persons within their jurisdiction. the right of every individual to an impartial decision on their case made solely based on the facts, the law and the evidence, free from outside bias, is protected by the independence of every judge. A fair, consistent, and impartial administration of justice depends critically on an effective, efficient, and independent judiciary.

As a result, judicial independence is a necessary component of democracy, the rule of law, and the right to due process.

JUDICIARY'S FUNCTION IN TRANSFORMATIVE CONSTITUTIONALISM

The court is playing a crucial part in the constitution's transformational constitutionalism. Just as an example the scope of judicial activism included everything from environmental pollution to the preservation of historical sites, from workplace sexual harassment to foreign adoptions, from exposing high-level government corruption to paying out compensation for FR violations and from the freedom to access information to the right to a free and public basic education.

THE JUDICIARY'S INTEGRITY IN UPHOLDING CONSTITUTIONALISM

Without a completely independent court to uphold it, there can be no such thing as the rule of law. Undoubtedly, a strong democracy is seen to be characterised by an independent and impartial judiciary. The ability of the judiciary to affirm the supremacy of the Constitution might be a powerful tool. The process known as judicial review was developed in Britain, where the courts were given the authority to oversee the use of public power. In the US, if an administrative authority's order or action violates the due process provision of the Constitution, the Supreme Court may overturn it. Similar to the United States, India does not have a single article that supports the idea of judicial review. Numerous articles, such as Articles 13, 32, 131 through 136, 142, 143, 226 or 246, can be used in India to start the judicial review process.

Therefore, the Indian court has consistently been engaged in upholding constitutional rights, responding whenever contacted and seldom declining to make a decision. Instead, it refers to a phenomenon when the judiciary deviates from its traditional adjudicative duty and takes on novel roles by engaging in policy matters that are typically the purview of the other branches of the government.

CONCLUSION

For judgments involving constitutional freedom, basic rights, and obligations of a natural person or legal entity within the jurisdiction for safeguarding constitutionalism, the judicial system bears the greatest duty. Every legal entity's entitlement to unbiased judgement in its case based on the legislation enacted by the legislature, as well asthe facts of the case and the foundation for the evidence without excessive influence or pressure is safeguarded by judges' impartiality from a District Court to a judge on the Supreme Court. A well operating judicial system is essential for the administration of justice to be fair, consistent, and effective.

REFERENCES:

1. https://www.ijlmh.com/paper/role-of-judiciary-for-upholding-constitutionalism/

1. https://www.legalserviceindia.com/legal/article-4829-role-of-the-judiciary-in-upholding-constitutionalism.html

[1] PREAMBLE OF THE CONSTITUTION OF INDIA
[2]ARTICLE 12 TO 35 OF THE CONSTITUTION OF INDIA
[3]ARTICLE 36 TO 51 OF THE CONSTITUTION OF INDIA
[4]ARTICLE 32 OF THE CONSTITUTION OF INDIA
[5]ARTICLE 5 OF THE CONSTITUTION OF INDIA
[6]AIR 1980 SC 1789.
[7] ARTICLE 14 OF THE CONSTITUTION OF INDIA
[8] AIR 1987 (1) SCC 362
[9]PREAMBLE OF THE CONSTITUTION OF INDIA
[10]Ibid
[11]AIR 1973 SC 1461
[12]AIR 1950 SC 25
[13]AIR 1995 SCC (1) 400
[14] AIR 1951 SC 458
[15] AIR 1965 SC 845
[16] AIR 1984 SC 802
[17] PREAMBLE OF THE CONSTITUTION OF INDIA
[18] ARTICLE 14 OF THE CONSTITUTION OF INDIA

CHAPTER VI

CORRUPTION IN INDIA{Author: Babanpreet Kaur}

"Corruption is a tree, whose branches are of an immeasurable length: they spread everywhere." Montesquieu[1]

Corruption is a global phenomenon that undermines economic development, political stability, and social justice. It is a complex problem that takes various forms and affects all sectors of society, from the government to the private sector and civil society. Corruption occurs when individuals or organizations abuse their power for personal gain, often at the expense of the common good. It can take many forms, such as bribery, embezzlement, nepotism, and cronyism, and it can occur at all levels of society, from petty corruption in everyday interactions to grand corruption at the highest levels of government.

The effects of corruption are profound and far-reaching, particularly in developing countries like India, where it is a significant challenge to economic growth and development. Corruption can lead to inefficiencies in the allocation of resources, distortions in markets, and a lack of trust in institutions. It also has a detrimental impact on social justice, as it often perpetuates inequalities and exclusion. In addition, corruption undermines the rule of law, erodes public trust in government, and can even threaten national security.Despite its negative consequences, corruption remains a pervasive problem in many parts of the world, including India.The government, civil society, and international organizations have made efforts to combat corruption, but progress has been slow and uneven. So, It is a major obstacle to economic development, social progress, and good governance. Corruption has become so deeply ingrained in the Indian society that it is often considered a way of life.

Facts and data on corruption in India

India ranks 86th out of 180 countries in Transparency International's Corruption Perceptions Index 2021, indicating a high level of corruption in the country. According to a survey conducted by the Centre for Media Studies in 2019, corruption in India has increased by 5% in the last year, with 51% of households believing that corruption has gone up in the country. The Central Bureau of Investigation[2] (CBI) registered a total of 3,925 corruption cases in 2019, up from 3,175 cases in 2018. The Comptroller and Auditor General (CAG) of India estimated that the government lost around Rs 1.76 lakh crore($24 billion) due to irregularities in government contracts between 2014 and 2018.

The Enforcement Directorate (ED), which investigates financial crimes and money laundering, registered 1,817 cases of money laundering in 2020-21, up from 1,197 cases in 2019-20.The Public Affairs Index 2020, which assesses governance performance in Indian states, found that the states of Kerala, Tamil Nadu, and Maharashtra were the least corrupt, while the states of Bihar, Jharkhand, and Uttar Pradesh were the most corrupt.Bribery is a common form of corruption in India, with a survey conducted by Transparency International in 2019 finding that 39% of Indians had paid a bribe in the last 12 months. The Prevention of Corruption Act, which is the primary anti-corruption law in India, was amended in 2018 to make the punishment for bribery more stringent, with a maximum imprisonment of seven years.

Causes of Corruption in India

- One of the key causes of corruption in India is the lack of transparency and accountability in government and public institutions. The absence of a robust legal and regulatory framework has made it easy for people to engage in corrupt practices without fear of being caught. As noted by former Prime Minister Manmohan Singh, "The root cause of corruption lies in the absence of transparency and accountability in government institutions."

- Socio-economic inequality is another major cause of corruption in India. The rich and powerful have access to resources and influence that the poor and marginalized do not. This disparity in access to resources and influence has created an uneven playing field, where those with power and influence can manipulate the system to their advantage.
- Political patronage: Many corrupt practices in India are linked to political patronage. Politicians use their power and influence to reward their supporters, and these supporters often engage in corrupt practices to maintain their supporters, and these supporters often engage in corrupt practices to maintain their positions of power and influence. As noted by former Chief Justice of India J.S. Verma, "Corruption has become a part of the Indian political and bureaucratic DNA. The nexus between politicians, businessmen, and bureaucrats is at the root of corruption in India."
- Culture of bribery: Bribery has become an accepted way of doing business in India. People often offer bribes to get things done quickly or to circumvent bureaucratic procedures.
- Lack of proper enforcement mechanisms:Even when laws against corruption exist, they are often not enforced properly. This allows corrupt individuals to get away with their actions and further encourages corruption.
- Weaknesses in the justice system:The justice system in India is slow and overburdened, which means that cases of corruption can take years to be resolved. This lack of timely justice encourages corrupt individuals to continue their activities. As noted by Indian economist and Nobel laureate AmartyaSen, "The Indian justice system is slow and inefficient, which makes it difficult to punish corrupt individuals in a timely manner."
- Lack of political will:The political will to fight corruption is often lacking in India. Politicians may themselves be involved in corrupt practices, or they may not want to alienate their supporters by cracking down on corruption.

Famous Case laws on corruption

- **Hawala case**

Vineet Narain v Union of India[3] case, also known as the "Hawala case," is a significant corruption case in India. The case involved allegations of corruption against several high-profile politicians, including the then sitting Prime Minister of India, P.V. Narasimha Rao. The case began in 1993 when a Jain hawala operator was arrested by the Enforcement Directorate (ED) for illegal money transactions. During the investigation, evidence was uncovered indicating that several prominent politicians had received large sums of money through hawala transactions, which are illegal under Indian law. In 1996, journalists VineetNarain and S. Balakrishnan filed a Public Interest Litigation (PIL) in the Supreme Court of India, seeking an investigation into the allegations of corruption. The PIL resulted in the court directing the Central Bureau of Investigation (CBI) to investigate the case and prosecute those found guilty. The CBI investigation uncovered evidence of corruption against several high-profile politicians, including P.V. Narasimha Rao, L.K. Advani, and SharadYadav. The investigation also revealed the extent of corruption in Indian politics and the nexus between politicians, businessmen, and criminal elements. In 1998, the Supreme Court of India delivered a landmark judgment in the case, directing the government to set up a special investigating team (SIT) to probe cases of corruption against high-level officials. The court also directed the government to establish a mechanism to insulate the CBI and other investigating agencies from political interference.

- **1992 Indian stock market scam[4]**

Harshad S. Mehta was an Indian stockbroker and businessman who was involved in a massive securities scam in the early 1990s. He was accused of using fraudulent means to manipulate the stock market, causing the stock prices of certain companies to rise artificially. This led to a huge rise in the stock market index, but eventually resulted in a crash in 1992. He was arrested by the Central Bureau of Investigation (CBI) in November 1992 and charged with several offences, including criminal breach of trust, forgery, cheating, and criminal conspiracy. The case against him was based on the findings of the Joint Parliamentary Committee, which had investigated the securities scam.Mehta filed a writ petition in the Supreme Court of India challenging the constitutional validity of the SEBI Act and the jurisdiction of the SEBI to regulate the stock market. The Supreme Court, in its judgment in the case of Harshad Mehta v. Union of India, held that the SEBI Act was constitutionally valid and that SEBI had the jurisdiction to regulate the securities market.Mehta was also charged with several criminal offences under the Indian Penal Code and the Criminal Procedure Code. The trial court found him guilty on several counts and sentenced him to rigorous imprisonment. Mehta challenged his conviction before the Bombay High Court, but his appeal was dismissed.Mehta then approached the Supreme Court, challenging his conviction and the legality of the investigation by the CBI. The Supreme Court, in its judgment in the case of Harshad S. Mehta v. State of Maharashtra, upheld his conviction and dismissed his appeal. The court held that the investigation by the CBI was legal and that Mehta had committed several criminal offences, including criminal breach of trust, forgery, and cheating.The case highlighted the need for better regulation of the securities market and the importance of investigating and prosecuting white-collar crimes. The case also demonstrated the role of the courts in upholding the rule of law and ensuring justice for all.

- **2G Spectrum Case[5] (2012)**

The 2G spectrum case is one of the most significant corruption cases in India's history. It involved the allocation of 2G spectrum licenses by the government in 2008 to several private telecom companies at rates much lower than their market value. The case alleged that this allocation was done in a corrupt manner, and resulted in a loss of revenue to the government amounting to billions of dollars. The 2G spectrum case led to the arrest of several high-profile individuals, including former telecom minister A. Raja, and several corporate executives. The investigation into the case revealed a complex web of corruption involving government officials, politicians, and business executives.The case was investigated by the Central Bureau of Investigation (CBI) and the Enforcement Directorate (ED), and went through several rounds of hearings in various courts. In 2017, a special court acquitted all the accused in the case, citing a lack of evidence. However, the verdict was later overturned by the Delhi High Court, which found that the lower court had erred in its judgment. In 2018, the Delhi High Court convicted a Raja and several other accused in the case, while also upholding the acquittal of others. The court imposed strict penalties on the convicted individuals, including fines and imprisonment.

Laws and regulations to prevent corruption in India

- The Prevention of Corruption Act[6]is the primary legislation in India that deals with corruption. The act was enacted to prevent corruption and punish those found guilty of corrupt practices. The act defines corruption as the act of a public servant or any other person abusing his or her position to obtain an undue advantage for himself or herself or for any other person. It criminalizes bribery, extortion, and misuse of public office for private gain. The act has provisions for the punishment of offenders, including imprisonment and fines. It also contains provisions for the confiscation of property obtained through corrupt practices. The act requires public servants to declare their assets and liabilities, and failure to do so can result in punishment. It also provides protection to whistleblowers who report corruption or wrongdoing. Under the act, a special court can be established to hear corruption cases. The act empowers the central and state governments to appoint special judges to handle corruption cases. However, there have been criticisms of the act, including its narrow definition of corruption and the need to strengthen enforcement mechanisms.

- The Indian Penal Code[7] (IPC) contains several provisions related to corruption. The IPC is a criminal code that contains provisions for the punishment of offenses such as bribery, extortion, and misuse of public office for private gain. Some of the key provisions related to corruption in the IPC are: Section 405[8] of the IPC criminalizes the act of a public servant or any other person who dishonestly misappropriates or converts for his or her own use any property entrusted to him or her. Section 415[9] of the IPC criminalizes the act of deceiving someone to gain an undue advantage. This provision is often used in cases of financial fraud and embezzlement. Section 463[10] of the IPC deals with forgery and it criminalizes the act of creating a false document with the intention of deceiving someone or committing fraud. Section 120B[11] of the IPC criminalizes the act of two or more people conspiring to commit an offense, including corruption. Section 171E[12] of the IPC criminalizes the act of offering or accepting a bribe to influence the outcome of an election. Overall, the Indian Penal Code contains several provisions that can be used to prosecute those found guilty of corrupt practices.
- The Whistleblowers Protection Act[13] is a law in India that provides protection to whistleblowers who report corruption or wrongdoing. The act was enacted to encourage and facilitate the disclosure of information about corrupt activities and to protect those who come forward to report such activities. Under the act, a whistleblower is defined as any person who makes a disclosure in good faith of an act or omission that constitutes an offense under the Prevention of Corruption Act, 1988 or any other law. The act provides protection to such whistleblowers from victimization, harassment, or discrimination. The act

establishes a mechanism for receiving and handling complaints from whistleblowers. It requires public servants to receive and act on complaints within a specified time frame. It also provides for the appointment of a competent authority to investigate complaints and take appropriate action. The act has provisions for the punishment of anyone who victimizes or discriminates against a whistleblower. It also allows for the compensation of whistleblowers who suffer losses or damages as a result of victimization or discrimination.

- The Prevention of Money Laundering Act[14] (PMLA) was enacted in India in 2002 to prevent and combat money laundering, which is the process of concealing the proceeds of illegal activities and making them appear legitimate. Money laundering is often associated with corruption as it is frequently used by corrupt individuals to hide the illicit funds they have obtained through bribery or embezzlement. The PMLA provides a legal framework to investigate and prosecute individuals or organizations involved in money laundering activities. The Act defines money laundering as a criminal offence and provides for stringent punishments including imprisonment and hefty fines. It also sets up a financial intelligence unit to track suspicious financial transactions and requires reporting entities such as banks, financial institutions, and other regulated entities to maintain records of their transactions and report any suspicious activity to the authorities. The PMLA has been used to investigate several high-profile corruption cases in India, including those involving politicians, bureaucrats, and businessmen.
- The Right to Information Act[15](RTI Act) is a powerful tool in the fight against corruption as it enables citizens to access information related to government functioning and hold public officials accountable. The RTI Act is applicable to all public authorities, including government departments, public sector undertakings, and institutions receiving government funding. Under the RTI Act, any citizen of India can file a request for

information from a public authority. The public authority is required to provide the information within 30 days of the receipt of the request, failing which, the applicant can file an appeal to a higher authority. In the context of corruption, the RTI Act can be used to obtain information related to government contracts, tenders, and other dealings. For instance, an applicant can file an RTI request seeking information related to the award of a government contract, including the names of the bidders, their financial bids, and the evaluation criteria used. This information can be used to scrutinize the award of the contract and check for any irregularities. Similarly, the RTI Act can be used to obtain information related to the functioning of government departments and agencies, including the allocation of funds, appointment of officials, and the use of government resources. This information can be used to hold public officials accountable for any instances of corruption or misuse of power. Moreover, the RTI Act provides for the imposition of penalties on public officials who refuse to provide information or provide false information. This provision acts as a deterrent to public officials who may be inclined to withhold information or provide misleading information.

- Companies Act[16]: This law requires companies to have internal mechanisms in place to prevent and detect corruption.

Measures to combat corruption

Addressing corruption in India requires a multi-pronged approach involving a combination of legal, institutional, and societal interventions. Here are some solutions that could help reduce corruption in India:

- **Strengthening anti-corruption laws:** The government should strengthen existing laws related to corruption, such as the Prevention of Corruption Act, and ensure that they are effectively enforced. The laws should also include provisions for transparency and accountability in public procurement, and protection for whistleblowers.

- **Enhancing transparency:** The government should promote greater transparency in public institutions, including publishing information related to government contracts, budgets, and expenditure. This can help reduce opportunities for corruption and increase public trust in government.
- **Reforming political funding:** The government should introduce reforms to regulate political funding and make the process more transparent. This can help reduce the influence of money on politics and curb corruption in the political system.
- **Promoting public awareness:** Raising public awareness about the negative impacts of corruption can help reduce tolerance for corrupt practices and increase demand for accountability. This can be achieved through public education campaigns, civic education programs, and media campaigns.
- **Strengthening institutions:** The government should invest in strengthening institutions responsible for combating corruption, such as anti-corruption agencies, the judiciary, and law enforcement agencies. This can involve providing these institutions with adequate resources, training, and independence.
- **Using technology:** Technology can be used to promote transparency and reduce opportunities for corruption. For example, e-governance initiatives can streamline administrative processes and reduce the need for intermediaries, reducing the scope for corrupt practices.
- **Encouraging citizen participation:** Encouraging citizen participation in decision-making processes and creating avenues for public feedback can help increase accountability and reduce opportunities for corruption.

Overall, addressing corruption in India requires a sustained effort and a commitment from all stakeholders, including government, civil society, and the private sector. A combination of legal, institutional, and societal interventions is necessary to tackle corruption effectively.

Conclusion

Corruption is a persistent problem in India that continues to hinder the country's progress and development. As the Nobel laureate economist AmartyaSen once said, "Corruption is one of the greatest challenges to economic and social development in India." However, there is hope that with sustained effort and a commitment from all stakeholders, corruption can be reduced and the country can move towards a more transparent and accountable society. As Mahatma Gandhi once said, "The only way to reform a society is to be reformed oneself." Therefore, it is up to all individuals to take responsibility and act with integrity to combat corruption and build a better future for India.

[1] https://thepoint.gm/africa/gambia/article/no-place-for-corruption-anywhere

[2] https://www.indiatoday.in/cities/mumbai/story/cbi-registers-case-against-two-officers-for-accepting-monetary-favours-2338735-2023-02-23

[3] VineetNarain& Others vs Union Of India & Another on 18 December, 1997

[4]Harshad S. Mehta vs Central Bureau Of Investigation on 21 September, 1998

[5]Subramanian SwamyvsA.Raja on 24 August, 2012

[6]The Prevention of Corruption Act, 1988

[7]Indian Penal Code, 1860(Act no. 45 of Year 1860)

[8] Sec 405. Criminal breach of trust [Indian Penal Code (45 of 1860)]

[9]Sec415. Cheating [Indian Penal Code (45 of 1860)]

[10] Sec 463. Forgery [Indian Penal Code (45 of 1860)]

[11] Sec 120B. Punishment of criminalconspiracy[Indian Penal Code (45 of 1860)]

[12]Sec 171E. Punishment for bribery [Indian Penal Code (45 of 1860)]

[13]Whistleblowers Protection Act, 2014

[14]Prevention of Money Laundering Act, 2002

[15]The Right to Information Act, 2005
[16]The Companies Act, 2013 (No. 18 of 2013)

CHAPTER VII

BIG DATA – DATA PROTECTION AND PRIVACY {Author: Alisha Gupta}

1. INTRODUCTION

With the expansion of technology, the innovations have reached at pinnacle of their maximum implementation in day to day working. Every individual is aware about major functionalities, processes, uses and importance of the technology in every field. The rapid growth of internet facilities has increased the use of more apps and social media platforms; people and businesses are now moving online which ultimately resulting in generating more datasets. The various digital or OTT platforms are attracting over a million of users on daily basis, which has scaled up the data generation more than ever before. Such huge quantity of datasets are handled, processed, controlled and stored in various devices; and this whole mechanism is regarded as "Big Data"[1]. It also includes the usage of various other statistical analytics; modern era technology such as machine learning; mining; artificial intelligence; digital statistics and others. It is very evident that 'Big data' is a next biggest thing in the world of IT sector (Information Technology), as now the individuals as well as the society at large are becoming aware about the potential power of such huge data on developing a business[2]. Nowadays, people are more vigilant about the powerful possibilities which can be originated by combining structured, unstructured and semi-structured data. The benefits of big data are becoming apparent in every day-to-day life of an individual and it spreads over every sphere such as predicting criminal behaviour, gene-based medical breakthrough, online maps, location-based hotels, gyms or clubs recommendations to the customers and many more.

However, with the maximum usage of big data all over the world, various general as well as legal challenges and concerns related to big data is also maximising immensely[3]. The data owners are now more conscious and vigilant about the growing unlimited hunger for data collection, its widespread use and significant abuse at the same time. They have concerns related to the data protection, their privacy, what all actions taken for the safety of their sensitive and personal data in the hands of big organisations. Although, the regulators are trying to enact laws that can answer all these questions, but yet there are no unified rules and regulations for protecting the data and privacy of the individuals.

2. DATA PROTECTION

When a common man uses a service or help; purchases a product at online shopping; registers for email; visits a specialist or doctor; pays the tax; enters into any legal agreement or contract or request service and many other day-to-day small transactions digitally, he is required to hand over some of his personal and sensitive information with a third party. Unintentionally, the data of the individual is being produced and collected by big entities so that they can enhance their business[4]. The only way to tackle this involuntary transfer of data is to implement more strong and stringent regulations for data protection involving effective legislations in order to decrease corporate as well as state supervision and minimise exploitation of the collected data.

The phrase "Data protection", in common sense, is defined as the laws enacted for safeguarding the personal and sensitive data of an individual[5]. In this fast growing modern world, in order to empower a common man, it isessential that laws for data protection must control and re-structure the actions taken by the private organisations and the government for collecting information of the individuals. While dealing with the concept of data protection, various crucial questions arises, such as, "Who had the right to access the given information?" "Was it stored accurately and precisely?" "Was it being gathered and circulated without their consent or knowledge?" "Could it be utilised to differentiate or infringe other fundamental rights of the individual?"[6]

Because of all the above stated questions and growing concerns of the common public, various data protection principles were introduced through frequent national and international consultations. "The *German region of Hesse* passed the first law in *1970*, while the '*US Fair Credit Reporting Act, 1970'* also enshrined various elements of data protection"[7]. "The US-led expansion of a '*code for fair information practices*' in the early 1970s which continued to shape various data protection laws today as well. Around this time only, the UK had established a well-known committee in order to review the threats given by several private organisations related to use of assembled information of the citizens. The committee of UKalso came to similar conclusion that data protection is need of the hour."[8] In the year 1980, "*Organisation for Economic Cooperation and Development"* (OECD) had circulated its directives and some principles, which involved the 'privacy concern' as well. Soon afterwards, the well reputable"*Council of Europe's Convention for the Protection of Individuals"* in relation to the '*Automatic Processing of Personal Data*' came into strength – which was again modernised and developed in the year 2018[9].

The 'Data Protection' and 'Data Privacy' are intrinsically connected to each other. All the individuals, as a general citizen or a consumer, are required to have such tools and mechanisms which may help them to enforce and implement their 'fundamental right to privacy' in order to protect their sensitive information from being misused and secure their information from any kind of exploitation or abuse[10]. Data protection is concerned with preservationof the individual's 'right to privacy' by implementing several obligations for handing over their personal data to any entity; the individuals are supposed to be provided with tangible rights upon their own data; and establishing such mechanisms of transparency, accountability and apparent obligations upon those organisations or agencies (whether public or private) which manage or embark on the analysation, examination and processing of data[11].

3. DATA PRIVACY

The expression "data privacy" has attained far more attention as compare to just the protection and security of data or information. In common terms, data privacy means that the data owners (in the capacity of customers or employees), must be aware aboutthe fact that big entities are collecting "what" personal data about them and "how" these entities are utilising this assembled data. In recent years, there were a number of high-status privacy violation and data-breach cases which had involved large amount of fines from the regulators of data protection. These high-profile cases had amplified the awareness among general public related to the significance of privacy of an individual and protection of their data from any kind of abuse. The "*European Union*" (EU) had accredited the "*General Data Protection Regulations*"[12] (GDPR), which provides a stringent legal framework and more firm standards for collecting and processing the assembled information about the individuals. It also regulates the privacy of an individual whose data is being collected by big companies. It providesvarious guidelines for the protection of data from any exploitation. Additionally, *GDPR* further works towards snowballingalertness and awareness among the general public related to the significance of complying with the data protection regulations[13].

The above mentioned data protection regulations are based on several key principles fundamentally. These set of principles establishes the foundation and backbone for ensuring privacy of individuals and protection of their data. The organisations (private or public) or the big commercial entities dealing with the collection and processing of big data, must adhere to these key principles in order to attain edge in the competitive market and enhance their businesses[14]. These principles deal with various aspects of data privacy, such as:

a. Lawfulness; fairness and transparency;

b. Responsibility and accountability of the entities;
c. Defined and lawful purpose of collecting data;
d. Maintaining data accuracy, integrity and confidentiality;
e. Handling personal and sensitive data with due diligence and extra care;
f. Data minimisation and storage limitations;
g. Risk mitigation and benefits assessment and many more.

The above stated principles are included in the *GDPR* as well. "*Article 5 of GDPR* specifically provides seven principles of data privacy and these key principles lie in the heart and soul of data protection administration. The principles are given at the very beginning of data protection regulations which should be complied strictly by all the organisations dealing with collection and processing of information of the common people". In case of failure to obey these set of regulations, defaulting party has to face harsh consequences and penalties from the regulators of the data privacy and protection of data"[15]. These key principles are mainly elaborated under GDPR and either directly or indirectly are included under privacy and data protection regulation of other countries as well. These are the guiding principles for processing the information collected by the big organisations[16].

4. CONSTITUTION OF INDIA AND PRIVACY

The honourable Supreme Court of India has recognised in plethora of cases that "*right to privacy*" is a sub-part of the widerfundamental rightcherished under Article 21 of Constitution[17]. The Indian judiciary considers the right to life and liberty as the core of all other fundamental rights available to citizens of India. "The magnitude of Article 21[18] has been extended to include various other rights and "right to privacy" is one such right included in the words "life and liberty" by courts[19].

The concept of privacy of individual and data organization which is prevalent at present, could be directly linked with the "*Fair Information Practice Principles*" (FIPP)[20]. The said Information

Principles are also observed by various intercontinental regimes, such as the "OCED Privacy Guidelines; APEC Framework or the nine National Privacy Principles" that are expressed in a report of the committee under the leadership of *'Mr. Justice A.P Shah'*. In 2012, the panel had proposed a comprehensive legal framework for protecting the privacy of data owners and safeguarding the personal or sensitive data which is being processed in various private and public spheres, on the basis of above stated principles. The panel had also recommended that commissioners for determining privacy issues are required to be established at Central and State level. The report by the panel had laid down "nine national privacy principles" which might be strictly observed while framing the laws on privacy[21].

The issue of 'right to privacy' came into contemplation before the vigilant eye of the Apex court, in the landmark case of "*K. S. Puttaswamy (Retd.) v. Union of India*"[22]. In this particular case the "*Aadhaar Card Scheme*" has been under question which is to be examined by the Supreme Court. The foundation of Aadhaar Card was based on gathering and aggregating the huge datasets with the help of biometric information of the citizens of India which can be used for various purposes by the govt. officials without taking permission from the data owners. The collection of biometrics would be considered as unwanted penetration into the fundamental "right to protection" of an individual.

The Apex court came to the conclusion in the year 2017 and clearly held that "right to privacy" or "privilege to security" is included under Article 21 of the Constitution as part of "right to life and personal liberty" of the individuals. The court in explicit words noted that the "Aadhaar Scheme" is a greatest threat and a serious incursion into the "right to privacy" of citizens and it has also the capability to create a state of surveillance, whereby each and every citizen of India may be kept under supervision by the govt. officials; regular inspection of this state may be obtained by generating life profile of the individual and it also has the tendency to track every movement of the citizens without their consent. The Act infringes the privacy and freedom of every individual, thus in a manner offends the "right to privacy" which was given an important rank under specific Articles 14, 19 and 21 of the Constitution.

5. **PERSONAL DATA PROTECTION BILL, 2019**

We all are aware that, there is no comprehensive legal framework in India which deals with the data privacy and the data protection specifically. "The legislation or the policies which are already existing under Indian laws are very narrow in its nature. These are: *Information Technology Act, 2000*; *Information Technology Rules, 2011*; *Right to Information Act, 2005*; various regulation governing telecommunications, banking sector, healthcare, insurance etc"[23]. All these legislations provide general process for gathering information, the usage of such data by the corporate entities. None of the legal framework deals specifically with the protection and safety of assembled data in India.

The legal experts of Justice A.P. Shah's committee had presented their inclusive report on October 16, 2012"[24]. After analysing this report in the year 2017, the "*Ministry of Electronics and Information Technology*" had set up another commission for comprehensively reviewing the privacy issues focusing mainly on the data protection. The Indian govt. had established this commission of experts under the guidance of honourable "*Mr. Justice B N Srikrishna*". The report by the commission was submitted in the mid of 2018[25]. The commission had advised the draft "*Personal Data Protection Bill, 2018*". After many discussions in the Parliament of India, the Bill was accepted by the cabinet ministry on 4 December 2019 as the '***Personal Data Protection Bill 2019***' and tabled it in the lower house i.e. the Lok Sabha on 11 December 2019"[26].

The preamble of the Bill expressly stated that the provisions are aimed to secure protection of personal and sensitive data of the individuals which is being collected by the public as well as private entities. It will also manage the relationship between data owners and the organisations collecting the data from them. The processing, analysing, and dissemination of the collected data is also taken care of under the Bill. Most importantly, it provides for the establishment of Data Protection Authority at centre level in order to regulate all the matters related to data protection and privacy of the data owners.

6. **CRITICISM AND WITHDRAWAL OF BILL**

Due to various defects in the provisions of the Bill, it was withdrawn by the Lok Sabha on August 3, 2022. "The Bill is withdrawn with a report stating that more broad and detailed version of the provisions may be presented in the Parliament in near future; which would cover maximum laws for protecting data and privacy of the data owners. It is reported by several sources that the govt. may introduce a "*Digital India Act*" which might replace "Information Technology Act, 2000" and would also cover the provisions for online business, data protection and privacy of data principals"[27].

The Bill of 2019 was having many flaws and it was even criticized by Mr. Justice BN Shrikrishna who was the founder of original bill. "He clearly stated that the provisions of the Bill has the ability to turn India into an '*Orwellian State*'; whereby the Central govt. is given power to exempt its agencies from the applicability of the provisions of Bill"[28]. "*The 'Orwellian State' term is used to represent draconian control of its citizens by a state as described in the novel 'Nineteen Eighty Four' by George Orwell*"[29]. He clearly stated that, "*They have removed the safeguards. That is most dangerous. The government can at anytime access private data of individuals or government agency's data on grounds of sovereignty or public order. This has dangerous implications*"[30].

There are many other critics having almost same views against the Bill. Mainly, the provisions related to data localization; lack of regulations for non-personal data; and exemptions given to the Govt entities; excess responsibility and answerability upon the social-media platforms; etc. became the key points for the criticism and the heated debate among the members of Parliament. The Bill lacks in including additional aspects of fast growing technology in India. Various deeper issues related to data security, privacy concerns, and data sovereignty requires reconsideration from the experts. "Thus, while dealing with all above stated issues a fresh and practical approach is required towards protection of data and right to privacy of individuals. More pragmatic and realistic contemplations should be taken by the experts committee about such data protection regulations and legal framework which may be designed to best suit the need of India and its citizens"[31].

7. CONCLUSION

"Big Data is indeed a buzzword, but it is one that is frankly under-hyped." – Ginni Rometty, a well-known American Business Executive.

'*Ginni Rometty*', the CEO of IBM (International Business Machines, American Multinational Company) had remarked that "*Big Data, Social-Media, and Data Analytics are three major areas which have the ability to give competitive advantages to the companies*"[32]. She had pointed out specifically that "data collected by the companies, will act as a foundation for company and in near future it will be considered as '*the next natural resource*' for that company". She further said that, "with the incoming '*tsunami of information*', those business entities which are able to utilise big datasets to their most benefits will make better and more objective calls"[33].

It is apparent that Big Data carries sufficient weight in the present world of innovation. The big data analytics is significant not only for private entities but also for the politicians, regulators and for customers as well. The regulations which are given by 'European Union' are playing crucial role in allowing more revolutions in big data analytics. But India, as a developing country is lacking behind in this specific area of technology. The privacy and data protection principles are required under Indian business models as well, as this will enhance the growth of Indian companies working in data analytics. "The major govt. initiatives in India such as 'Digital India Programme'; 'Smart cities mission'; 'Central Monitoring system'; 'Aadhaar platform'; 'Big data banks'; and many more requires the attention, because these initiatives have used big data on large scale"[34]. It is pertinent to note that India does not have any specific law dealing with privacy issues, in order to provide security against any kind of arbitrary interference into the rights of an individual, therefore it becomes very complex to secure the information collected by the authorities. Hence, the codified and comprehensive regulations for protecting data and securing privacy rights is a need of the hour.

[1] AI Community, "Advantages and Disadvantages of Big Data", August 5, 2021; *available at:* https://towardsai.net/p/l/advantages-disadvantages-of-big-data

[2] C. Kypreos and D. Rotman, et.al., "Big Data Analytics & Privacy: How to Resolve This Paradox?", 2017; *available at:* https://www.compact.nl/en/articles/big-data-analytics-privacy-how-to-resolve-this-paradox

[3] Jamie Henriquez, "Big data: Six critical areas of legal risk", October 6, 2014; *available at:*https://www.techrepublic.com/article/big-data-six-critical-areas-of-legal-risk

[4]Ibid.

[5] David Banisar, "National Comprehensive Data Protection/ Privacy Laws and Bills 2018", *available at*: https://papers.ssrn.com/sol3/papers.cfm?abstract_id=1951416

[6] Ibid.

[7] Robert Gellman, "Fair Information Practices: A Basic History", April 2017, *available at*: https://bobgellman.com/rg-docs/rg-FIPshistory.pdf

[8] Ibid.

[9] Protocol amending the Convention for the Protection of Individuals with regard to Automatic Processing of Personal Data (ETS No. 108), 128th Session of the Committee of Ministers, 18 May 2018, CM(2018)2-final. *Available at*: https://search.coe.int/cm/Pages/result_details.aspx

[10] Thomas A Singlehurst et al, 'ePrivacy and Data Protection', CitiGroup, March 2017, p4. *Available at*: https://www.citibank.com/commercialbank/in sights/assets/

docs/ePrivacyand Data.pdf

[11] Privacy International, "State of Privacy", *available at:* https://www.privacyinternational.org/reports/state-ofprivacy

[12] Jake Frankenfield, "General Data Protection Regulation (GDPR) Definition and Meaning", Nov 11, 2020; *available at:* https://www.investopedia.com/terms/g/general-data-protection-regulation-gdpr.asp

[13]Ibid.

[14]Data Protection Commision, "Principles of Data Protection", 2018; *available at:*

https://www.dataprotection.ie/en/individuals/data-protection-basics/principles-data-protection

[15] Data Protection Commision, "Principles of Data Protection", 2018; *available at:*

https://www.dataprotection.ie/en/individuals/data-protection-basics/principles-data-protection

[16] UHI, "The Seven Principles", 2019; *available at:*https://www.uhi.ac.uk/en/about-uhi/governance/policies-andregulations/data-protection/the-seven-principles

[17]*Kharak Singh v State of UP*, AIR 1963 SC 1295.

[18]Constitution of India. Art. 21. Right to Life and Personal Liberty.

[19]*People's Union of Civil Liberties v. the Union of India*, (1997) 1 SCC 318.

[20]R. Rajagopal v. State of Tamil Nadu, 1994 SCC (6) 632.

[21] Report of the Group of Experts on Privacy (Chaired by Justice A P Shah, Former Chief Justice, Delhi High Court), *available at:* http://planningcommission.nic.in/reports/genrep/rep_privacy.pdf

[22] (2015) 8 SCC 735.

[23]Rishabh, "A Critical Analysis on Data Protection and Privacy Issues in India" *available at:*

https://www.legalserviceindia.com/legal/article-2705-a-critical-analysis-on-data-protection-and-privacy-issues-inindia.html

[24]Ibid.

[25]ShrutiDhapola, “Personal Data Protection Bill 2018 draft submitted by Justice Srikrishna Committee: Here is what it says”, *available at:* https://indianexpress.com/article/technology/tech-news-technology/personal-dataprotection-bill-2018-justice-srikrishna-data-protection-report-submitted-to-meity-5279972/

[26] “Union Cabinet clears Personal Data Protection Bill: Major takeaways from Cabinet meet”, The Economic Times, Dec. 4, 2019, *available at:* https://economictimes.indiatimes.com/news/economy/policy/union-cabinet

[27] Sameer Avasarala, "Advent of a new-era Digital India Act – Key aspects to look out", Lakshmikumaran&Sridharan Attorneys; *available at:* https://www.lakshmisri.com/insights/articles/advent-of-a-new-era-digital-indiaact-key-aspects-to-look-out

[28]Surabhi Agarwal, "Joint parliamentary committee wants more time to submit data bill note", *The Economic Times*, March 25, 2020.

[29]Ibid.

[30]MeghaMandavia, “Personal Data Protection Bill can turn India into ‘Orwellian State’: Justice BN Srikrishna”, The Economic Times, Dec. 12, 2019.

[31]ArindrajitBasu and Justin Sherman, “Key Global Takeaways From India’s Revised Personal Data Protection Bill”, *available at:* https://www.lawfareblog.com/key-global-takeaways-indias-revised-personal-data-protection-bill

[32]Andrew Grill, “IBM CEO Ginni Rometty believes big data and social will change everything – how about other CEOs?” March 11, 2013 *available at:* https://actionablefuturist.com/2013/03/ibm-ceo-ginni-rometty-believes-bigdata-and-social-will-change-everything-how-about-other-ceos/

[33]Ibid.

[34]BuddhadebHalder, “Privacy in India, in the Age of Big Data”, 2020, *available at:*

https://www.apc.org/sites/default/files/Privacy-in-India-in-the-Age-of-Big-Data.pdf

CHAPTER VIII

AFSPA: ITS GENESIS AND JUDICAL INTERPRETATION {Author: Navjot Kaur}

INDIA, as we know, is considered as a nation which has absorbed the ideals of democracy in the truest sense, a nation which gives due importance to the rights and liberties of its citizens. The government is indeed by the people, to the people and for the people. Indian culture is a product of assimilation of diverse cultures and religions that came into existence in the Indian sub-continent over time. One of the abiding factors of it is the respect for the dignity of an individual and striving for peace and harmony in the society. However, it is difficult to imagine that in a country like ours, exists a law which makes a mockery of the basic Human Rights and that is the draconian law, as mostly recognized, of Armed Forces Special Powers Act. It is a much maligned law which stands out because of its misuse and arbitrary powers given to the security forces which go against the basic principles of rule of law.

In the last six decades, India has been sworn to an increase in instances of violent conflict which have been variously bestowed as terrorism, insurgency, militancy, proxy war and armed rebellion. Our biggest challenge today, as for most of the world, is terrorism and militancy. We have had some successes in the past, but in every case, we have had to preserve over many years affecting the economic development of the victim state. While terrorism was largely a local phenomenon until recently when terrorist networks have taken advantage of the communication revolution to develop transnational links, making terrorism a global threat. Terrorist outfits now have enough ability to cooperate with each other and build operational links in the form of supply of arms, logistical and even operational support without necessarily sharing ideological bonds. They also obtain support from organized crime outfits to further their destructive objectives.

There are numerous logical and irrational causes of terrorism. Some course of events slowly and quietly in favourable conditions may turn into systematic terrorist activities. Some cause of terrorism in the modern world can be political, social, economic or religious. Recent boom in communication satellite, a world under network of broadcasting media like radio, television, cable t.v., internet, e-mails, fax machines have largely facilitated the activities of publicity seeking terrorists It also gives mode to other fanatics to join the terrorist gangs. Though the root causes of terrorism, in most of the cases, are internal but for its long time continuance, support from across the borders of the country is obvious. As in the case of secessionist challenges from their minority communities in many countries, particularly of third world, the internal factors create the objective conditions for its growth, rise and maturity, and the external factors provide the insurgents with finances, weapons, training and logistic support that are instrumental for prolonging the terrorism.

Threats of insurgency have also increased in our country in the last three decades. When an irregular armed force tries to fight with a stronger force by sabotage and harassment, it is called a state of insurgency. So, insurgent may be called as a person who takes part in an armed rebellion against a constituted authority (especially in the hope of improving the conditions). Insurgents use all possible means, political resources, propaganda and foreign assistance as means of spreading violence against the targeted political system, which they disapprove or consider illegitimate. The main reasons for insurgency in a country are peculiar geographic and demographic configuration of the country, its immediate neighbourhood, infiltration across the borders facilitated by the ethnic and religious coalitions of the population along the international frontiers. Various countries of the region are facing rivalries due to discrepancies in economic conditions and the resources. So, to achieve equality, even unfair and unethical methods are employed.

As the tensity between a state's prerogative and individual rights amplifies, it articulates the question of whose security and whose rights are at stake in this political climate. National security or state security is all about protecting the state from the potential or real enemies who may be citizens or alien to the state. And it is obvious, as reminded by experts, that whenever the state is to be protected from an external enemy, rights of citizens are often sacrificed in the interest of defensive measures. But in order to tackle the menace of terrorism and insurgency and to ensure the human rights of the citizens alongside, the law enforcement agencies have to be supported with an appropriate legal framework, an adequate training infrastructure, equipment and intelligence.

A unique global instrument ever entered and agreed by all member states of United Nations was The United Nations Global Counter-terrorism Strategy, 2006; with the objective to enhance national, regional and international efforts to counter terrorism. Counter-terrorism refers to a combination of practices, tactics, techniques, and strategies that governments, armies, police departments, and military contractors adopt to prevent terrorism or respond to threats posed by terrorists It includes two essential elements:

1. Ensuring that citizens are safer from terrorist threats by taking multifaceted security measures-domestically as well as internationally;
2. Neutralizing terrorists through arrests, prosecutions, raids, and military actions.

It also enlists a reasonable degree of cooperation with other governments on matters ranging from international financial situations and strategic partnerships to intelligence sharing.

The National Security Strategy of India also covers a strategy for fighting terrorism and insurgency. Its discourse is based on ensuring protection of life and property for all creating and maintaining a secure environment for individuals to develop to their fullest potential. Any threat which could slow down this process has to be considered a threat to national security. Many anti-terrorism laws have been passed from time to time to combat the evil of terrorism, insurgency and militancy situations arising in the country.Many special laws were also framed by few states in this regard.

Under normal circumstances law and order, in India, is a provincial (state) subject, but in case of failure and helpless of a state and its civil power, the union or central government may declare that particular state, wholly or a part of it, to be disturbed area under the existing special laws and send armed forces in aid of civil power. The UN Charter also gives the victim states the right to respond with military force in the event of an "armed attack", but does not define the term "armed attack".

During such operations army not only fight against the militants and insurgents but also tries to reassure the civilians about their security when they are extremely tensed and neglected due to inadequate civil administration. Large scale civic action programmes are undertaken by the army along with anti-terrorist operations. In Nagaland and Manipur, army has formed an Army Development Group for this purpose.

Armed Forces or military of a nation is created to safeguard its boundaries against external aggression and maintain its integrity and sovereignty. The Indian armed forces are quite unique. They are the only apolitical forces of the third world and are looked upon as a nationalist institution. Yet no one, including the political leaders, is clear about the role played by the armed forces, especially the army, in the modern Indian society. One of the basic features of a democratic system is civilian control over military. But, politicians and bureaucrats have no understanding of it and its implications. It should mean the control exercised by the Defence Minister under the guidance of the Prime Minister. In reality, the Indian armed forces are controlled by civilian officials in the Ministry of Defence. The bureaucracy has become the front end of the defence establishment, exercising control and supervisory functions, and acting as gatekeepers.

The Indian soldier has to struggle through a hard life and also have to face an ineffective system of grievance redress. A retired officer writes...

"The internal security operations are man-power intensive and Army is considered to be having enough tendency in restoring law and order situations".

Army has been involved almost on a permanent basis in internal security duties since the 1980s.Though Army need not to be employed when the civil administration is intact and is functioning properly. Long-term deployment of the army can only be justified in two situations: firstly, when the insurgents are strong or well armed to be tackled by the state police or CPMF; and secondly, when in the border states they have external support and safe havens across the international borders.

GENESIS OF AFSPA

The AFSPA – like many other controversial laws – is of a colonial origin. The AFSPA was first enacted as an ordinance in the backdrop of the Quit India Movement launched by Mahatma Gandhi in 1942.A day after its launch on August 8, 1942, the movement became leaderless and turned violent in many places across the country. Shaken by the massive scale of violence across the country, the then **Viceroy Linlithgow** promulgated the Armed Forces (Special Powers) Ordinance, 1942.This Ordinance practically gave the Armed Forces a “license to kill” when faced with internal disturbances.

However, the genesis of AFSPA can be traced back to the post-independence period, where India has witnessed many secessionist movements and has long suffered from extremist unity of the country. In order to curb the secessionist activities of the militants, the Indian government under the leadership of Pandit Nehru implemented the AFSPA in 1958.But, Civil Liberties Organization have dubbed AFSPA a colonial instrument modelled on the Armed Forces Special Powers Ordinance, 1942. They have accused the Indian government for violating the international standards of human rights given in the International Bill of Human Rights and affirmed in the Indian constitution. Pointing to this, recently, the Chief Justice of India said that

"merational community could not fault India if it chose to enact a lough or a stringent law to tackle the menace of terrorism".

The Indian Parliament has enacted three different acts under AFSPA for different regions:

1. Armed Forces Special Powers (Assam and Manipur) Act, 1958

2. The Armed Forces (Punjab and Chandigarh) Special Powers Act, 1983

3. The Armed Forces (Jammu and Kashmir) Special Powers Act, 1990

Though these acts are not uniform in nature. Initially, the Armed Forces Special Powers (Assam and Manipur) Act, 1958was brought to tackle the Naga problem to maintain peace situation against the acts of Naga armed opposition groups-both Issac Muivah and kaplang factions of the Nationalist Socialist Council of Nagaland. Originally, it came into being as an ordinance in 1950 and within 6 months was repealed and passed as an act to be applied to Assam and Manipur. But, the reorganization of the north-eastern states paved the way for the amendment of the AFSPA to be applied to each state differently according to the situations prevailing in each state. Though, after 57 years, the Naga-problem is far from resolve.

However, recently, AFSPA has been removed from several districts of three North-Eastern States. AFSPA is being removed from 15 police station areas in seven districts of Nagaland; 15 police station areas in six districts of Manipur; and 23 districts entirely and one district partially in Assam. According to the government, the step is a "result of the improved security situation and fast-tracked development due to the consistent efforts and several agreements to end insurgency and bring lasting peace in Northeast". At the same time, AFSPA was extended in three districts of Arunachal Pradesh by 6 months.

Moreover, after 18 years, the state government of Tripura decided to withdraw the act from the entire state in the year 2015 in view of significant taming of militancy-related incidents in the state. However, Tripura is not the first state to completely do away with AFSPA. It was withdrawn from the State of Mizoram in the 1980s and Meghalaya in 2018. Additionally, it was enforced in Punjab also in 1983 to suppress the secessionist movements and lasted for 14 years until 1997.

Furthermore, its application is bit complex in Jammu and Kashmir which has its own Disturbed Areas Act, 1992 and has lapsed in 1998. But, the government justifies its action to still declare it as a disturbed area under section 3 of AFSPA. However, pointing towards the Northeastern states, India's Defence Minister, Rajnath Singh, stated that these states have created atmosphere of peace and stability which helped the Home Ministry to remove AFSPA from various parts of these states. Therefore, if similar situation of peace and tranquillity prevails in the Union Territory, the Central Government will certainly consider to remove The Armed Forces (Jammu and Kashmir) Special Powers Act, 1990.

CONSTITUTIONAL VALIDITY OF AFSPA

Legislative Competency

While examining the legislative competency of Parliament to make a law what is required to be seen is whether the subject matter falls in the State List which Parliament cannot enter. If the law does not fall within State List, Parliament would have legislative competence to pass the law by virtue of the residuary powers under Article 248 read with Entry 97 of the Union List and it would not be necessary to go into the question whether it falls under any entry in the Union List or the Concurrent List. Prior to the Constitution (Forty-Second Amendment) Act, 1976, the relevant entries were as follows:-

List I-Union List, Entry 2:Naval, Military and Air Forces, any other armed forces of Union.

List II-State List, Entry 1:Public Order (but not including the use of Naval, Military or Air Force or any other armed force of the Union in aid of the Civil power).

By the Constitution (Forty-Second Amendment) Act, 1976, Entry 2A was inserted in the Union List. The said Entry read as follows:-

"Deployment of any armed force of the Union or any other force subject to the control of the Union or any contingent or unit thereof in any State in aid of the civilpower."

Entry 1 of the State List was amended to read as under;-

"Public order (but not including the use of any Naval, Military or Air Force or any other armed force of the Union or of any other force subject to the control of the Union or of any contingent or unit thereof in aid of civil power. "

By the said amendment Article 257-A[1] was also inserted which was however deleted by the Forty-Forth Amendment in 1976. But no change was made in any of the entries in the State List.

The Armed Forces Special Powers Act, is a law with respect to "Public Order and falls under Entry I of the State List but on the other hand, submitted that the central Act does not fall under any entry in the State List and, as originally enacted in 1958, it was a law made under Article 248 read with Entry 97 of the Union List and alley the Fort-Second Amendment of the Constitution it is a law falling under Entry 2A of the Union List.

The expression "in aid of the civil power" in Entry 1 of the State List and Entry 2A of the Union List implies that the deployment of armed forces of the Union shall be for the purpose of enabling the civil power in the state to deal with the situation affecting maintenance of public order which has necessitated the deployment of armed forces in the state. The word "aid" postulates the continued existence of the authority to be aided. This simply means that the civil power that has to be aided continues to function. The said forces operate in the concerned State in cooperation with the civil administration to deal the situation effectively and restorenormalcy.

Constitutionally Valid Legislation Being Passed Under Article 355

When the conflicts in the civil society are left unchecked for a long time, they escalate into destructive threats to the nation. So, to deal with such situation our Constitution makers added the provisions to aid the civil administrators of the State to bring normalcy in the disturbed areas, by deployment of armed forces in the insurgency affected area. The Union and the State government has been given the power to declare any area to be disturbed area and allow the army to operate there for fighting the insurgency situation prevailing there under Armed Forces Special Powers Act. The act was enacted for the by the Union government under the power given to it under Article 355 of the Indian Constitution. The APSPA can be justified on the ground that as per Article 355 of the Indian Constitution, it is the duty of the Union to protect States against external aggression and internal disturbance and to ensure that the government of every State is carried on in accordance with the provisions of the Constitution. It took fifteen years for the Supreme Court to uphold the Constitutional validity of the AFSPA. AFSPA is essential to combat insurgency and protect our borders and if it is repelled, along with which "immunity" granted under the AFSPA to army personnel against acts/omissions commissioned as part of their "official duty" will go away, army has to be withdrawn from 'disturbed areas' because without immunity, army cannot act/ operate against insurgent since they will fear prosecution in court of law for their acts and this will affect their morale. The constitutional history behind the passing of the present day Indian Constitution could be referred here to discuss the importance of Article 355 and then to establish the validity of the Act.

Our constitution has been established under the Government of India Act, 1935, which was repealed and modified many a times but it still remains the framework on which the present Constitution is based. So, reading these provisions in the light of GOI Act, 1935 we can find that section 45 and 93 of the Act deals with Failure of constitutional machinery in the federation and the provinces. These were enacted because one section of the congress party had declared its intention to enter the legislatures only in order to wreck them from within. Since that Act fell for short of the party's demand for full-self government. These sections were not covered under the emergency powers but under separate chapter entitled 'provisions in case of failure of constitutional machinery' in the Federation and the Provisions respectively. The language of the sections reproduces that the power is conferred on the President to ensure the proper functioning of the Constitution in the discharge of the duty laid upon the Union to protect every state that against external aggression or internal disturbance and to ensure that the government of every State is carried on in accordance with the provisions of the constitution.

The Act covers four sections, which were in substance fundamental rights though not so called, which were not suspended even during proclamation of emergency. Such proclamation does not even enable the legislatures to enact laws which, but for the emergency, they would not have been able to make. For the clear understanding of the nature of the powers now grouped together in Part XVIII of constitution, the emergency provisions would have been placed in the chapter on the distribution of legislative powers; and if it was intended to authorize suspension of fundamental rights and the making of laws, that provisions should have been inserted either in Part III of the Constitution or incorporated as a proviso to the Article on the distribution of legislative power-since fundamental rights act as fetter on legislative power.

Article 227-278 in the draft Constitution titled 'emergency provisions. Repeated changes were made. After considerable discussions in the drafting committee, Dr. Ambedkar introduced the new draft, in which Article 277A (present day Article 355) ran as follows:

"It shall be the duty of the Union to protect every State against external aggression and internal disturbance and to ensure that the government of every state i[2]s carried on in accordance with the provisions of this constitution".

INTERPRETING THE PROVISIONS OF THE ACT: CASE ANALYSIS

AFSPA is a law that has been passed with an intention to provide assistance to the administration in the protection of the civilians against the insurgents. But, time and again it has been criticized of giving excessive powers in the hands of the armed forces giving them enough scope to misuse the powers. Therefore, while interpreting the provisions of the Act the judiciary has to take in view the present situation by using various tools available to interpret so as to extract the grammatical, literal or the strained meanings whichever suits the varied situations. Hence, interpretation must be done in the light of the facts and circumstances of each case.

Indrajit Barua Vs State of Assam and another

In this case[3], a writ petition under Article 226 was filed by the petitioner in the Gauhati High Court challenging certain legislative actions of the State of Assam and the Parliament and consequent administrative actions of the Governor of the State of Assam. The legislative competence of the Assam legislature and the Parliament was challenged regarding the Assam Disturbed Areas Act, 1955 and the Armed Forces (Assam and Manipur) Special Powers Act, 1958 read with the Armed Forces (Assam and Manipur) Special Powers (Amendment) Act, 1972.Section 2, 3, 4 and 5 were questioned being against the Articles 14, 19 and 21 of the Constitution. The lagal issue in this case was whether there is arbitrariness as to the definition of disturbed areas and public order as per Section 2, 3 and 4 of the AFSPA, 1958.The court decided that the lack of precision to the definition of a disturbed area was not an issue. In support of this judgement following reasons were given by the court:

- **Section 2** of the AFSPA defines disturbed areas as an area which is for the time being declared by notification under Section 3 to be a disturbed area. As per **Section 3** the power to declare the area to be disturbed lies with the Governor of that State or the Administrative of the Union Territory or the Central Government, in case there exists such a disturbed or dangerous situation that the use of armed forces in aid of the civil power is necessary.

It was further submitted that the act of declaring an area to be disturbed is without any basis and irrational. In other words, it is whimsical and fanciful amounting to arbitrariness. Any law or procedure which leads to inhumane or degrading treatment, as accordingly is permitted or contemplated by Section 4 of the Assam Act and Section 4 of the Central Act, cannot stand the test of reasonableness and absence of arbitrariness and as such will not constitute procedure established by law within the meaning of Article 21 of the Constitution. Therefore, it can be concluded that as far as the terms "public order" and "disturbed areas" are concerned, there is still much vagueness regarding the definitions of the two terms in the Act. However, this decision of the Delhi High Court has been referred to in many later decisions since it was one of the first cases that attempted to interpret the provisions of the said Act. Since the declaration depends on the satisfaction of the Governmental Official, the declaration that an area is disturbed is not subject to judicial review.

Naga People's Movement of Human Rights Vs. Union of India

In this case[4] Writ Petitions were filed under Article 32 of the Constitution, the validity of the Central Act and the State Act as well as the notifications issued under the said enactments declaring areas in the State of Assam, Manipur an Tripura were challenged on the ground that it violates Articles 14, 19 and 21 of the Constitution of India. Allegations have been made regarding infringement of human rights by personnel of armed forces in exercise of the powers conferred by the Central Act. The notifications regarding declaration of disturbed areas have ceased to operate. The main legal issues were:

-Whether Section 2(b) defining "disturbed area" is vague in as much as it does not lay down any guidelines for declaring an area to be a disturbed area.

-Whether Section 3 entails that there is no requirement of a periodic review of a declaration issued under and that a declaration once issued can operate without any limit of time.

-Whether the conferment of power to issue a declaration under Section 3 of the Central Act on the Governor of the State is invalid since it amounts to delegation of power of the Central Government.

-Whether as regards Section 4, there is no justification for having a special law as the Armed Forces Special Powers Act because adequate provisions are contained in the Cr.P.C. to deal with a situation regarding the use of armed forces in aid of civil power.

-Whether the conferment of powers to a junior officer under Section 4 Created the likelihood of the powers being misused and abused.

-Whether the protection given under Section 6 virtually provides immunity to persons exercising the powers conferred under Section 4 in as much as it extends the protection also to "anything purported to be done in exercise of the powers conferred by this Act".

The validity of the Armed Forces Special Powers Act, 1958 was upheld. The Hon'ble Supreme Court of Indian in the case of Naga People's Movement of Human Rights, etc. v. VOL, held that the powers given to the officers of armed forces, including the non-commissioned officers, under Section 4 and 5 of the AFSPA are not volatile of Article 14, 19 or 21 of the Constitution. While acting under such powers the officers should use minimal force required for effective action against the person/persons acting in contravention of the prohibitory order.

The term "disturbed area" defies any definition. A disturbed area has to be adjudged according to location, situation and circumstances of particular case. As the term implies, only such area would be disturbed area where there is absence of peace and tranquility. For an area to be declared as 'disturbed area" there must exist a grave situation of law and order on the basis of which the Governor/Administrator of the State/Union Territory or the Central Government can form an opinion that area is in such a disturbed or dangerous condition that the use of armed forces in aid of civil power is necessary. Therefore it cannot, therefore, be said that an arbitrary and unguided power has been conferred in the matter of declaring an area as disturbed area.

The words "for the time being" used in Section 2(b) imply that the declaration under Section 3 has to operate only for limited duration and not indefinitely. It is no doubt true that there is as such no requirement that the declaration should be reviewed periodically. But, as the legislature intended to declare the area disturbed for the time being when there is grave situation of law and order only, so it carries within it an obligation to review the gravity of the situation from time to time and the continuance of the declaration has to be decided on such a periodic assessment of the gravity of the situation.

Under Section 3 of the Central Act there is no delegation of power of the Central Government to the Governor of the State. The power to issue a declaration has been conferred on by parliament on three authorities, namely the Governor of the State, the Administrator of the Union Territory, and the Central Government. Moreover, the issuance of a declaration, by itself, would not oblige the Central Government to deploy the armed forces of the Union. After such declaration the decision to deploy the armed forces is taken by the Central Government. Therefore, the conferment of power on the Governor of the State to make the declaration under Section 3 cannot be regarded as delegation of the power of the Central Government.

Masooda Parveen Vs Union Of India & Ors.

In this case[5], the deceased ChulamMohi-ud-din Regoo, was an advocate enrolled and practicing in the High Court of Jammu and Kashmir before the Srinagar Bench. In addition to his practice he was also a small-time businessman trading in saffron, but on account of certain factors, sustained heavy losses on which his creditors approached local militants for help in recovering the amounts due to them. As a consequence of this pressure, Regoo shifted from his village Chandhara to Sopore and remained away for a period of two years from 1992 to 1994 and then returned as there was in the meanwhile a decline in the strength of the militants. It appears that some militants who were working along with the Army got him arrested on 61 October, 1994 on the allegation that he was a Pakistani Trained Militant(PTM) and he was kept in custody for about three months and then released, and on return continued to follow his vocations in a peaceful manner. On I" February, 1998 some surrendered militants along with a unit of the Army (17 Jat) reached Regoo's home in Chandhara at about 8:30 p.m. and searched his house but found nothing incriminating therein. He was nevertheless taken to the Lethapora Army Camp, the Head Quarters of the 17 Jat, and tortured mercilessly leading to his death where after explosives were placed on his dead body and then detonated to camouflage the murder. It is further the petitioners' case that the morning after the incident, his body was handed over to the police and was thereafter subjected to a very casual and cursory post mortem examination. It is in these circumstances that a case for compensation etc. has been made on the plea that the deceased had left behind an indigent family comprising of his widow and four children. In this writ petition, a prayer has been made that the respondent- Union of India be called upon to pay compensation and to provide a job on compassionate grounds for the custodial death of Ghulam Mohi-ud-din Regoo.

The Hon'ble High Court decided that we cannot ignore the fact that many in Kashmir who have gone astray are Indian citizens and it is this situation which has led to this incident. We do appreciate that a fight against militancy is more a battle for the minds of such persons, than a victory by force of arms, which is pyrrhic and invariably leads to no permanent solution. We cannot ignore the fact that in this process many unfortunate incidents do occur which raise the ire of the civil population, often exacerbating the situation, and the belief of being unduly targeted with a feeling in contrast of the law order machinery that it is often in the dock and called upon to explain the steps that they have taken in the course of what they rightly believe to be the nation's fight. We, however, believe that the examination of a complaint, and the provisions of an effective redressal, mechanism preferably at the hands of administration itself, or through a court of law if necessary, is perhaps one of the most important features in securing a psychological advantage. We also understand that in an investigation of this kind based only on affidavits, with a hapless and destitute widow in utter despair on the one side and the might of the State on the other, the search for the truth is decidedly unequal and the court must therefore tilt just a little in favour of the victim.

General Officer Commanding Vs. CBI and An. and Additional Director General Vs. Central Bureau Investigation

This case[6] involves two criminal appeals numbered 257 of 2011 and 55 of 2006. As the facts and legal issues involved in both the appeals are similar, the decision has been made by a common judgment.

On 22.2.1994, the 18th Battalion of Punjab Regiment was deployed in Tinsukhia District of Assam to carry out the counter insurgency operation in the area of Saikhowa Reserve Forest. The said Army personnel faced the insurgents who opened fire from an ambush and in the process of return fire, some militants died. Upon the continued search of the Battalion at the place of encounter, bodies of the militants along with arms and ammunitions were recovered. An FIR was and the local Police also visited the place and investigated the case. Under the Army Act investigation was conducted by the Army and their version of inquiry was found to be true and the finding was recorded the counter insurgency operation was done in exercise of the official duty. Two wait petitions were filed before the High Court alleging that the killings were done in a fake encounter. The CBI filed a chargesheet in the Court of Special Judicial Magistrate against the Army personnel and the Court issued a notice to the Appellant to collect the chargesheet. The Appellant has requested the said Court not to proceed with the matter as the action had been carried out by the Army personnel in performance of their official duty and thus, they were protected under the Act 1958 and in order to proceed further in the matter, sanction of the Central Government was necessary. This was rejected by the Court and aggrieved Appellant filed a revision petition before the High Court which was also rejected by the High Court. Hence, this appeal. The legal issues involved in this matter were:

-Whether the term 'institution' mentioned in S. 7 of the 1990 Act therein means filing, presenting, submitting the chargesheet in the court or taking cognizance.

-Whether the court can proceed with the trial without previous sanction of the Central Government.

It was held that the conjoint reading of the relevant statutory provisions and rules make it clear that the term "institution" contained in Section 7 of the Act 1990 means taking cognizance of the offence and not mere presentation of the chargesheet by the investigating agency. The court cannot proceed with the trial without a previous sanction of the Central Government under the 1990 Act in the present case. The option is given to the competent authority in the Army to decide as to whether the trial would be by the criminal court or by a Court Martial. In case the option is made to try the case by a Court Martial, the said proceedings would commence immediately. In case the option is made to try the case in the Criminal Court the CBI shall make an application to the Central Government for grant of sanction.

CONCLUSION

Being the largest Democracy of the World India is rightly expected to respect the basic principles of Human rights and International Humanitarian law. The AFSPA is essentially an emergency legislation and therefore, its temporal scope of application should be limited and clearly defined. However, before making any change in the Act, the government must understand the soldier's loyalty to the country, unprotesting and unsung, he toils on for his own Country. Whenever Army is deployed in the area of insurgency or an area declared as a 'disturbed area', for the effective functioning of the members of armed forces and to raise their morale to do the patriotic duty of securing the land and its people, they need a proper law redressal mechanism. They need special legal protection and powers in the areas where they operate. Efficient system should be there to protect the rights of the soldiers who are putting their lives in danger to serve and protect the country.

Though it is unfair and incorrect on the part of political authorities and social media to put pressure on the army officials deployed in such areas, at the same time the need of the hour is to include the areas declared as "disturbed areas" to the mainstream by establishing peace in such areas. The political leaders in these areas need to assess the security situation and resolve such issues through a consensus in unified command instead of making sensitive security issues a public agenda.

[1]*257-A Assistance to States by deployment of armed forces or other forces of the Union.—Omitted by the Constitution (Forty-fourth Amendment) Act, 1978, s. 33 (w.e.f. 20-6-1979).*

[2]*Shiva Rao, "The Framing of India's Constitution-A Study", pg.812*

[3]*Indrajit Barua Vs. State of Assam and another, AIR 1983 Del. 514*

[4]*Naga People's Movement of Human Rights Vs. Union of India, AIR 1998 SC 431*

[5]*Masooda Parveen Vs Union Of India & Ors. (2007)4 SCC 548*

[6]*General Officer Commanding Vs. CBI and An. and Additional Director General Vs. Central Bureau Investigation; AIR 2012 SC 1890*

CHAPTER IX

LAW OF DIVINE ONENESS {Author: Manju Kumari}

Understanding, the 12 Universal laws shows us how to master life on all levels i.e., energetically, spiritually, emotionally, mentally and physically. They gives us insights into what we can do to achieve our goals of this existence of earth and universe. But it's important to understand all the universal laws one by one to raise harmony in life. So, let's comprehend the first Law of Divine Oneness brings Harmony to all Universal Laws.

Divine law is any body of law that is perceived as deriving from a transcendent source, such as the will of God – in contrast to man- made law to secular law. According to Angelos and Rudolph, divine laws are typically perceived as superior to man-made laws, sometimes due to an assumption that their source has resources beyond human knowledge and human reason. Believers in divine laws might accord them greater authority than other laws, for example by assuming that divine law cannot be changed by human authorities.

Here, **LAW** means the rule which is enforceable by the creator of the universe and **ONENESS** is defined as state of being one and whole. Therefore, the law of Oneness is defined as we all are interconnected through our creation by a creator, we all are one manifestation of the creator.

Wilder said, "Every single atom inside of you is connected in some way, shape, or form to the rest of the universe you move through."

This means that everything we do has a ripple effect and impacts the collective not just only ourselves.

Eckhart tolle said, "...In the sea on land. The air it is the universe delights in in creating this multiplicity of forms. And it delights in experiencing. Itself through all those forms..."

What is Spiritual Oneness?

The term Oneness is a term which is often used interchangeably with "non-duality" or "non-dual awareness – has traditionally been considered a state in which a person experiences consciousness in its true form as utterly devoid of subject–object distinctions.

Spiritual oneness is our birthday as we all are the children of the God. Deep down, you know this. I know this. We all know this. Something about it resonates deep within us. Oneness is our destiny. Therefore, we have to go beyond the senses, beyond duality to find Oneness.

How does the Law of Divine Oneness works?

If we think of the cycle of life. You are born, you grow old to the end of your time on earth. As the saying goes, and dust becomes dust. We are all created from the same single cosmic boom. We all have the same essence, the basis for life, flowing within us; our molecules and atoms constantly interacting with one another. In other words, you return to the earth from which you came.

It is that same ground that we grow our food on and from which our plants get their nutrients. Essentially, the connection we have on earth finds its way back to us in one form or the other. But it goes beyond the physical.

All things in the universe have a link to each other. Our existence is like a circle, and it is impossible to live a solitary life. Our Collective Consciousness and shared universal energy bind us to everyone and everything.

Practice: When you are standing in front of a mirror, take a moment to look straight into your eyes. Say "AHUM BRAHMASMI" (a-hum-brah-mass-me) either silently or out loud, which means "I am the universe" or "I am the totality." This is your soul reflecting back to itself and reiterating its unity. This should be done at least once a day, or whenever you see yourself in the mirror.

How do you practice Oneness?

13 ways by which an individual can achieveoneness –

1. Meditate and connect with the Divine Source

2. Spend time in nature
3. Conscious Breathing
4. Self-awareness and understanding of thoughts, emotions, actions, reactions and choices you make
5. Mantra chanting – AUM (OM), AHAM BRAHMASM, AHAM PREMA
6. Activate 7 Chakra of body
7. Observe everything around
8. Practice silence and look inside
9. Join Spiritual Community or spiritual people
10. Try compassion and gratitude
11. Yoga and exercise
12. Read spiritual content
13. Spiritual Practices and affirmations

How to Use the Law of Divine Oneness to Manifest What You Want?

Collective Consciousness means this universal energy that connects us. We are all conscious, so together, we make up the Collective Consciousness. The inventions the world has seen have become a reality because of one thing – they are a manifestation of people's desires. The more people with similar thoughts, the easier and faster these thoughts become a reality.

Every thought, action, words, beliefs etc. impact our Collective Conscience and existence. The significance of this is that you influence the type of life you lead and your circumstances. You have the control of whether you live a miserable judgmental or full of understanding joyous life. Whatever you dedicate your mind and thoughts to is what you manifest. If you harbour thoughts of happiness, peace, abundance, wealth, and good health, you attract them into your life.

Therefore, the whole divine sound is the cause of the manifestation. Just like a paper start burning after constant focus of sun rays by way of magnifier so here you also have to follow this focused concept for manifesting whatever you want. After consistent practice of affirmations on day to day life you start becoming more aware of your thoughts and your surroundings then you start to notice relationships between what you think and what manifests itself in your life. Soon after, positive statements/ affirmations they will lead to manifestation, which is the end game of the entire affirmations of the manifesting process. By the use of affirmations as a tool to get what we want by believing in ourselves, our power to make our dreams come true by the magic of manifestation. With continuous practice, you can manifesting things into your life and start to feel like having a magic power.

"As you sow in your subconscious mind, so shall you reap in your body and environment."-*Joseph Murphy*

Affirm: I trust the Universe. It gives me exactly what I need at exactly the right time. Everything works out perfectly for me. I am creating my dream life.

Affirm: I am always spiritually, emotionally, mentally, physically, financially powerful and abundant.

Affirm: "I welcome High vibrational thoughts and feelings into my experience. I move with the Divine Energies and allow **Miracles***to happen in my life. Thank you God".*

How to manifest what you want by understanding of Law of Divine Oneness?

1. Understand 12 Universal Law of Universe
2. Connecting with Supreme God
3. Enhancing virtues of Soul and raise the vibrations
4. Practice Positive Affirmations and repeat 3-7 times a day
5. Understand yourself and believe in yourself
6. Start journaling and try visualisation method
7. Be clear about what actually you want
8. Acknowledge and appreciate your present and small things in life
9. Trust the process
10. Acceptance and surrender is the key
11. Rid of limiting beliefs and resistance
12. Watch and listen Positive contents

Therefore, the Law of Oneness teaches that we are all linked. We all share the same energy and we all can manifestation a beautiful life together.

Everything is Connected and Law of Divine Oneness

According to the Law of Divine Oneness, *the whole universe is inter-connected.* Nothing lives on its own in its little bubble. Like one perfect formula we have deduced as humans to be the key to understanding the universe. Everything is energy. Everything is a vibration. Everything is operating at a certain frequency. And if we can learn how to control our particular frequency and manipulate it for the better, we can begin to ascend to the next level of consciousness.

— **EckhartTolle** At the deepest level, an 'open heart' is spacious presence, in which the sense of separateness between yourself and the 'other' dissolves and there is the recognition of **oneness**, of shared consciousness. That recognition is love.

Everything is Energy and Energy is everything. The German dramatist and thinker Gotthold Lessing observed that -"In nature everything is connected, everything is interwoven, everything changes with everything and everything merges from one into another."

- *Body = Intelligence = Mind = Information = Energy = Consciousness = Spirit = Supreme God. The human body, plant and all physical things are made up of matter and energy. It's all the same thing. It's all ONE thing and everything is energy.*

Therefore, the Law of Oneness explains that every individual, every situation, and everything in the world is connected to each other.What someone else thinks or does may affect your life in some way and vice versa, even if you don't know the person at all.

What is the Legal Aspect of Universal Oneness?

Human rights are rights inherent to all human beings, regardless of race, sex, nationality, ethnicity, language, religion, or any other status. Human rights include the right to life and liberty, freedom from slavery and torture, freedom of opinion and expression, the right to work and education, and many more. Everyone is entitled to these rights, without discrimination.

International Human Rights Law

International Human Rights Law lays down the obligations of Governments to act in certain ways or to refrain from certain acts, in order to promote and protect human rights and fundamental freedoms of individuals or groups.

One of the great achievements of the United Nations is the creation of a comprehensive body of human rights law—a universal and internationally protected code to which all nations can subscribe and all people aspire. The United Nations has defined a broad range of internationally accepted rights, including civil, cultural, economic, political and social rights. It has also established mechanisms to promote and protect these rights and to assist states in carrying out their responsibilities.

Even, Human Rights Day is observed every year on 10 December — the day the United Nations General Assembly adopted, in 1948, the Universal Declaration of Human Rights (UDHR). The Universal Declaration of Human Rights (UDHR) is a milestone document in the history of human rights. As Article 1 to 30 prioritize dignity of human over rights. Dignity is the foundation of all human rights. Because every human being has intrinsic worth, they deserve to be treated with the utmost respect and care. Former UN rights chief ZeidRa'ad Al Hussein called these opening words "perhaps the most resonant and beautiful words of any international agreement." They underline that "human rights are not a reward for good behaviour," as he put it, but the entitlement of all people at all times and in all places.

The UDHR has been translated into more than 500 languages- the most translated document in the world - and has inspired the constitutions of many newly independent States and many new democracies. Some provisions are reproduced as under:

Article 1- Free and equal

All human beings are born free and equal and should be treated the same way: - All human beings are born free and equal in dignity and rights. They are endowed with reason and conscience and should act towards one another in a spirit of brotherhood.

Article 3- Right to life

Everyone has the right to life and to live in freedom and safety:- Everyone has the right to life, liberty and security of person.

Article 7- Right to equality before the law

The law is the same for everyone and should be applied in the same manner to all:- All are equal before the law and are entitled without any discrimination to equal protection of the law. All are entitled to equal protection against any discrimination in violation of this Declaration and against any incitement to such discrimination.

5 most important takeaways from understanding the Law of Divine Oneness are following:

1. We Are Not Separate Entities
2. Everything We Do Has an Effect on The World as we all are energy beings.
3. Our Collective Consciousness is a Powerhouse to manifest a beautiful and peaceful world.
4. A bigger Picture from the broad spectrum can be seen and the illusion of the individuality can be dissolved.

5. Law of Divine Oneness brings harmony to all Life laws as we are all God's children

Hence, the Law of Divine Oneness provides the fundamental understanding that we are all connected and our existence is same.

Now make full use of your ability to inspire, motivate, or excite the one you love and live your life with the consciousness of oneness.

CHAPTER X

A STUDY OF LAWS RELATING TO THE ACCOMPLICE WITNESS {Author: Navneet Bhathal}

An Accomplice is a person who takes part in the crime and helps another in the commission of the crime. An offence committed by more than persons and every individuals who takes part in the guilty act is an Accomplice. A witness who is participating in the commission may give denial for the part of the crime but it is upon the court after consideration of the evidence as whether he is competent for an Accomplice or not. An accomplice deals within the provisions of Indian Evidence Act, 1872 and The Criminal Procedure Code 1908. Evidence is an efficient part of the trial and helps to clear that whether a crime is committed or not. Benthem says, “any matter of fact, the effect, tendency or design of which is to produce in the mind a persuasion affirmative or dis-affirmative of the existence of some other matter of fact.”[1] To an common person the accomplice evidence is untrustworthy as the person is always an interested and infamous witness but the evidence is necessity for the justice of the other accused.

Who is an Accomplice: Meaning and Definition:

Accomplice word is not defined under the Indian Evidence Act, 1872 or any other law. However, in judicial terms the word has been interpreted in its various judgments.In *R.K.Dalmia v. Delhi Administration,*[2] that a person who voluntarily takes part or aids in the commission of a crime for which the accused is facing trial is an Accomplice. He is a particepscriminis and in the case where he provides testimony against the co-partners in crime for a pardon provided by the court, the accomplice is known as an approver. As per *Ramaswamy v. R,*[3] an accomplice is an individualwho is guilty-associate in the act or who sustain such a relation to the criminal guilt that he can be jointly tried with the principal criminal.

According to the New Oxford Dictionary, "accomplice may be called as a complice, meaning an associate in guilt, a part in crime,"[4]

History Relating to Accomplice:

In Canada, the Criminal Law is covered under Criminal Code which is a Federal Statute. The concept of Accomplice has been repealed by the parliament in Canada. In the Statute, new concept was introduced namely being a party to an offence. In R v. Greyeyes[5], an individual can become a party to an offence where they encourage the principal with acts, words and intend to encourage.[6]

In United States, in Criminal Law aiding and abetting is defined in the law. The person who helps and encourages someone for carried out the illegal acts. The person who is accessory to the guilty act.

Degrees of an Accomplice:

There are different categories of accomplices based on the participation in the crime.

- Principal in the First Degree: is a person who commits a crime with qwnswlf or through the party who is innocent. It is not necessary that only one person may be considered Principal, there can be more than one in an criminal act who are principal in Ist Degree.
- Principal in the Second Degree: A person in the Second Degree, who actually helps the other individual to commit a guilty act while in the presence of main accused.
- Accessories before the Fact: An Accessories before the fact is a person who help, counsels, connives at, encourages or procures someone to the commission of the crime. It is not important that physical presence required of the person at the place of act. The person helps the others to commit the criminal act.
- Accessories After the Fact:The person who helps to someone after the individual has committed the crime. That person was

charged for the Accessory after the Fact. Example: Hiding someone after the committing of crime. The person gives the space to person knows that he has participated in the crime. He helps to someone to escape from the arrest of police. They can become the accomplice as they participated in crime in some or other way.

Provisions under Different Laws:

Evidence Act:

Section 133 Accomplice: with regard to the competency of the Accomplice, Section 133 of the Indian Evidence Act says, "an accomplice shall be competent witness against an accused person; and conviction is not illegal merely because it proceeds upon the uncorroborated testimony of an accomplice."

As per Dr. J.K. Malik,[7] he was analyses the various texts, opinions of the authors by saying that accomplice should be considered as a competent witness as the term has never defined in the Indian Evidence Act, 1872 under Section 133 or under Section 114 Illustration(b) and in Criminal Procedure Code.

Section 114 Illustration (b): That an accomplice is unworthy of credit, unless he is corroborated in material particulars;[8]

After reading the Section 133 read with Section 114 illustration (b), it is clear that corroboration is the most necessary fact with respect to the accomplice. The rule regarding to the corroboration is a rule of prudence not a rule of law. With the combined reading of these two sections that a conviction based on the uncorroborated testimony of the accomplice is not illegal but it is dangerous to rely upon the evidence of the accomplice. It is important that at the time of conviction, a caution must be considered of the evidence of the accomplice.

In **R v. Baskerville**[9], declared that "there is no doubt that uncorroborated evidence of an accomplice is admissible in law. But it has been long a rule of practice for the judge at common law to warn the jury of the danger of convicting a prisoner on the uncorroborated testimony of an accomplice, and in discretion of the judge, to advise them not to convict merely upon such evidence, but the judge should mentioned the jury that it is within their province legally to convict upon such confirmed evidence."

Criminal Procedure Code:

Section 306, Section 307 and Section 308 of the Code of Criminal Procedure deals with the tender to pardon, the main purpose is to take the evidence of the person who is involved in the guilty act whether directly or indirectly with some conditions. Court of Session[10]or by the Court of Special Judge appointed under the Criminal Law Amendment Act, 1952 is the authorities to deal with the matter to tender pardon.

Judicial Decisions:

In **State of Maharashtra v. Abu Salem Abdul Qayyum Ansari & Others**[11], The Apex Court decided on the question of cross-examination of an approver that whether the accused has a right to cross-examine the accomplice/approver whose pardon has been withdrawn by the court. The Hon'ble Supreme Court held that-

"An accomplice who has been given the pardon by using the Section 306 and 307 of the Code of Criminal Procedure gets the protection from the Prosecution. The person who is called the witness of the guilty crime, he must have fulfill the conditions mentioned in the above said sections and making a true and full disclosure of the circumstances that is in his knowledge about the particular act and with regard to the any person whether about the principal or abettor. If an person fails to fulfill the conditions or suppress any material thing within his knowledge and fail to comply within the terms that has been made while tender the pardon, and the prosecution given the certificate under Section 308 of Criminal Procedure Code to that effect, the protection given to the approver or accomplice is lifted."

The settled law is that an approver is a competent person against an accused. But, when the court uses the evidence of that person, must have caution and prudence taken while giving the punishment of the evidence of that approver. The corroborated is required with the evidence. The reliability of the evidence must have considered from the facts and circumstances of the case:

The law laid down by the Apex Court with regard to the evidentiary value of the accomplice is that:-

i. That there must be corroboration with the material particular of the statement of Approver.
ii. That the conviction made on the uncorroborated testimony of the accomplice is not considered as illegal, but the corroboration is not required in the cases where the circumstances of the case suggest that the corroboration may be dispense with.
iii. When the combined reading of the bot sections 133 and 114 illustration (b) of the Evidence Act, an accomplice is a competent witness to give evidence but it will be unsafe if the conviction is made solely on the evidence of that accomplice. Though, the conviction on evidence of the accomplice is not illegal.
iv. The law with the accomplice is same in India as England.
v. That when the evidence given by the accomplice is held trustworthy, it must be shown that the story given by the approver must implicate him in such a way as to give rise to conclude the guilt beyond reasonable doubt. The corroboration is based on the rule of caution not on the rule of Law.
vi. That for the corroborated evidence, the court must look out the version of the Approver and then find out that whether there is other evidence to corroborate and give assurance to that version of the facts.

Parkash Alias Ajayan etc. v. State of Kerala[12], "The Kerala High court says that mere an accused is suffering from the disease of epilepsy, it does not make sense that he is not competent witness to give evidence of any fact. The person who is under an epileptic attack condition on certain occasionscannot considered a person to whom tender of pardon under Section 306 cannot be made. The main purpose of the Section 306 is that to obtain evidence from a person who is directly or indirectly connected with the crime or connected to prevent someone from the punishment of the crime and escape a person. That person cannot be termed as incapable of tender of pardon."

The court view in case of **Sarwan Singh v. State of Punjab**[13], "the court in this case receive a Double Test theory. In this case the third accused was tried for murder for the brother of first accused under Section 302 of the Indian Penal Code with the other two accused namely Harbans Singh and Gurdiyal Singh. Third accused i.e. Banta Singh become an approver later on against the other two accused. Thereafter, the other accused was convicted on the evidence given by the approver along with other corroboration material facts. Therefore, the evidence given by the Accomplice is subject to the corroboration evidence."

Evidentiary Value of an Accomplice:

Evidence plays an important role in the trial and it is necessary that the accused must have given a fair trial. Evidence is explained by the Benthem, any matter of fact, the tendency or design of which to produce in the mind a dis-affirmative or affirmative of the existence of other material fact. The conviction made solely on the basis of the evidence of the accomplice is not illegal. The rule deals with the rule of caution that must have corroboration of the other material facts with the story of the approver. It is much needed for that no injustice is done with any accused as the approver is also a part of the crime at one time and for that it is must that corroboration is required.

Conclusion:

The witness is mush needed aspect for the trial. While a conviction is made on one individual's statement who is also a part of the act the court should read the both section i.e. Section 133 and Section 114 illustration (b) of the Indian Evidence Act. These sections says it is not illegal that a conviction is made on the evidence of the accomplice as he is a competent witness, but some precaution must be there for conviction on the statement of witness as rule of prudence says that it is totally unsafe for an accused to convict. The evidence of the accomplice must be dealt with carefully as he has a motive to shift the guilt upon someone else and he hopes for pardon and favours the prosecution.[14] The nature of the corroboration is vary with the fact and circumstances of the each case.

Suggestions:

- There must be a definition of the Accomplice or Approver in the Indian Evidence Act, Indian Penal Code or in any other law. So, anyone can understand the aspect of the Accomplice.
- That one combined section is required for the evidentiary value of the accomplice along with the corroboration.
- An author Dr. J.K. Malik [15] given the suggestion in his journal that the witness must fulfill the conditions of Section 118 and 120 of the Indian Evidence Act, 1872. As he is in the part of the crime, he does not become an immoral person for his whole life.

[1]Benthem Ev.,17

[2]1962 AIR 1821

[3]14 MLJ 226

[4]KailashMissar v. Emperor, AIR 1931 Pat 105

[5](1997) 2 SCR 825.

[6]http://En.wikipedia.org

[7]Journal of the Legal Studies, Vol.XXXVI

[8]Indian Evidence Act, 1872.

[9](1916) 2 K.B. 658

[10]The Code of Criminal Procedure, 1973

[11]2003 Supreme Court cases (Cri) 1243

[12]2009 CrLJ 2930.

[13]1957 SCR 953

[14]Barkat Ali v. The Crown (1916) P.R No. 2 of 1917 Cr.

[15] Journals of Legal Studies, Vol XXXVI

CHAPTER XI

COPYRIGHT LAWS: HISTORICAL RETROSPECT {Author: Heena}

What is worth copying is worth protecting.[1]

INTRODUCTION

Copyright is a form of intellectual property right, protecting original works of authorship including literary, dramatic, musical, and artistic works, such as poetry, novels, movies, songs, computer software and works of architecture. Copyright according to Section 14 of the Indian Copyright Act, 1957 means, the exclusive right to do or authorize others to do certain acts in relation to 1.literary, dramatic, musical and artistic works. 2. Cinematograph films. 3. Sound recordings. [2]According to section 13 of the Act, copyright shall subsist throughout India only in the above classes of work.

Thus, copyright is the right to copy or reproduce the work in which copyright subsists, basically. A copyright provides its holder the right to restrict unauthorized copying and reproduction of an original expression. Reddy, J. has given a celebrated statement about owning of the copyright in *Gramophone Co. v. Birender Bahadur Panday*[3]: "An artistic, literary or musical work is the brainchild of the author, the fruit of his labor and so, considered to be his property. So highly is it prized by all civilized nations that are thought worthy of protection by national laws and international conventions."

In ancient Roman law, in works of genius & invention, as in painting on another man's canvas, the canvas is given to the painter, but not if it is only mechanical writing. It is the creator of the work who is entitled to have it. Original literary compositions cannot be published without the consent of the author and make profit. In ancient days creative writers, musicians and artists wrote, composed or made their works for fame and recognition rather than to earn a living. There is a sea change in this attitude in the modern times. People create works of this type with the intention of commercial application. These works, which were determining factors of personal status and scholarship during the earlier times, have become the economic assets of the creators.

These works have become economically important and their misuse has also increased. This has led to large-scale piracy of copyrighted works. Developments in the area of information technology have added new dimension to the large-scale piracy that has been going on unabated. Difficulty in identification of the piracy is coming in the way of complete elimination of piracy.

The rationale behind providing protection against infringement of copyright is that no one should be allowed to appropriate the fruits of another's labor whether it is tangible or intangible. Infringement means the interference with, or violation of the right of copyright of another; it takes place when a person other than the owner or author does something, which is the exclusive right of the owner or author. Infringing copy means reproduction without a license by the owner of a literary, dramatic, musical or artistic work, copy made of a cinematograph film, recording of sound recording, or a cinematograph of such film of such programs or performance in relation of which broadcasts, reproduction right or performer's right subsists. Infringement can be divided into primary infringement and secondary infringement. This type of infringement of copyright is popularly known as piracy.[4]

The word' Piracy 'comes via Latin word *Pirata* which was initially used for sea- robbers. Piracy, in the light of intellectual property, means the copying or reproduction of the property of the copyright owner for profit without his permission or proper authority. Some people believe that the term" piracy" is an easy connotation. But, it's the act of criminals who usually move to a greater extent in an organized way, engaged in imitating of products of other people's talents, skills, ideas and source of investments.

The technological development in the field of printing, music, communication, entertainment, computers, VCR, magnetic tapes etc. put a strain in the minds of intellectual property owners all over the world. All these have created extreme pressure for the expansion of protection of ideas and improvement of legal machinery against "piracy" and collective administration of rights. These have made the "Piracy" a global issue.

Moreover, the society has understood the value and need of the copyright law and because of this, every country, whether it's large or small, developing or developed has framed its own copyright law and are gradually amending it to bring it in conformity with the changing needs of the society.[5]

DEVELOPMENT OF LAW OF COPYRIGHT

The necessity of extending to the creator of literary works a suitable reward for his labors has long been recognized and cannot seriously be questioned.[6]The earliest recorded historical case law on the right to copy took place in557A.D.It involved Saint Columba, who while on a visit to the monastery of his former teacher, Abbot Finnian, copied the latter's Psalter; Finnian demanded the return of the copy and getting no satisfaction referred the dispute to the King, who ruled in his favor; "to every cow her calf and consequently to every book its copy".[7]

It was only with the invention of printing that allowed the easy and inexpensive duplication of paper works that the need of copyright protection was felt and hence, the copyright law was firstly introduced in United Kingdom in response to the need to protect the new printing trade against the unauthorized copying of books (piracy).

Initially, the copyright law applied only to the copying of the books .Over time, other uses such as translations and derivative works were made subject to copyright and copyright now covers a wide range of works, including maps, performances, paintings, photographs, sound recordings, broadcasts, motion pictures and computer programs etc.

Following is a brief study of law of modern law of copyright and its historyi.e.to see how it has developed from its origin to the present day position:

1. INVENTION OF THE PRINTING PRESS

The rights of literary works involving published works were not at all protected until the invention of printing press by Guttenberg in Germany in 1436.That was the time when copyright originated. As a result of the printing machines, the booksellers were able to copy author's manuscripts at a much faster rate.

Profits from the sale of books help the book- sellers to recover the costs of both author's manuscript and printing press.[8] Previously, someone would have to write the complete manuscript for making a copy, which from the commercial angle was not at all profitable .Printing allowed for multiple exact copies of work, leading to a more rapid and widespread circulation of ideas and information. From the beginning, copyright laws have been driven more by the economics of publication than by the economics of authorship. The first known copyright appeared in Italy.

The craft of printing was introduced in Rome and Venice by the end of 1460s.A number of privileges were allowed by Venice in terms of import of franchise ,exclusive licenses to print or sell an entire class of books, prohibition of import of books printing abroad and patents for the improvement of printing and typography. As the focus was on printing books in public domain, the rights of authorship were not considered important.[9]

An early statute of Richard III in 1483 encouraged the printing of books, and allowed their importation, but this statute was repealed 50 years later on protectionist grounds, it being alleged, in the preamble of the repealing statute in 1533, that such a marvelous number of printed books were imported into the realm to the prejudice of the King's natural subjects who have given themselves so diligently to learn and exercise the said craft of printing that at this day there be within this realm a great number cunning and expert in the said science or craft of printing as able to exercise the said craft in all points as any stranger in any other realm or country.

A similar plea was urged on behalf of the bookbinders who having no other faculty wherewith to get their living, be destitute of work and likely to be undone, except some reformation herein he had .As the member of printers increased in England, the King assumed a prerogative of granting printing privileges, and the earliest copyright protection took the form of printers‘ licenses granted by the sovereign to regulate the book trade and to protect printers against piracy. These privileges became a source of considerable profit to the Crown and used as an instrument of censorship by the authorities.

2. CENSORSHIP AND PRIVILEGES:

Within a few years after the introduction of printing, European states began to adopt legal measures to deal with consequences of this development. The simplest way to control the distribution of printed material, and protest local printing industries against piracy and foreign import, was to introduce control of the printing presses, so that the state authority would know what was being printed and by whom.

The state authority took unto itself the sole right of printing, and the authority to grant permissions to print. The control was exercised through general regulations providing that nothing could be printed without state's (or academic or ecclesiastical) authority, and by issuing decrees or ordinances authority particular persons to print and sell books of certain classes, or copies of particular works. These instruments are generally described as "privileges", in the sense of legislative instrument referring to a particular person as distinct from the community at large.

The turning point in the history of copyright was reached when authors in general, as opposed to particular individuals named in privileges, were granted rights to reproduce their works. The printing privileges were apparently the Decrees issued by the State Councilors' of Venice in the fifteenth century. The republic of Venice granted its first privilege for a particular book in 1486.[10] It was granted to a printer (Johannes of Speyer, by Decree of September 18, 1469), conferring an exclusive right to carry on the art of printing.

The second of these privileges was granted to an author (Marc Antony Sabellico, by Decree of September 1, 1486), conferring the exclusive right of author in printing of one of the author's named works. The 1486 Decree is the first recorded instance of the formal grant of an author's right to an author. The distinction between the first two recorded privileges is of much importance, the beneficiary of the 1469 privilege was a printer, given a monopoly to exercise a certain production method and may be likened to a patent. The beneficiary of the 1486 privilege was the author himself. Generally the privileges systems were of two classes:

(1) Those issued by the sovereign, as part of the royal prerogative, and

(2) Those issued by legislative and official bodies under the general powers of the state.[11]

In 1493, the Venetian cabinet gave Daniel Barbara an exclusive 10 year grant of propriety rights for the publication of the book authored by his deceased brother .Such cases were very few and copyrights by and large were issued to the publishers of books written by others. This was an interesting aspect of copyrights.

The first general copyright law in the world came in the form of a decree issued by the Venice Council around1545 which prohibited the printing of any work without the permission of the author.

3. CHARTER OF STATIONER'S COMPANY

From the early years of the first copying industry-printing- a pattern of exploitation had been developing: an entrepreneur, whose calling was typically that of "stationer", became the principal task risker; he acquired the work from its author (if he was not reprinting a classic) and organizing its printing and sale. The stationers (forefathers of modern publisher) were the chief proponents of exclusive rights against copiers. Certainly their own practices, their guild rules, their terms on which they dealt with authors insisted upon this exclusivity; their regime for "insiders" became a source of trade customs from which general rights against "outsiders" might be distilled.[12]

In this objective, the stationers early found an ally in the Crown. In 1534, they secured protection against the importation of foreign books; and in 1556, Mary, with her acute concern about religious opposition, granted the Stationer's Company a charter under which it was forbidden, amongst other things, to print contrary to any ordinance, prohibition or commandant in any of the statutes or laws of the realm, or any injunction, letters patent, or ordinance set forth, or to be set forth by queen's grant, commission or authority.[13]

The decree forbade anything to be printed which had first not been licensed and entered in the stationer's register, a record book maintained by the Stationer's Company of London. The company had been given a royal charter in 1557 to regulate the various professions associated with the publishing industry, including printers ,bookbinders, booksellers, and publishers in England .The Register itself allowed publishers to document their right to produce a particular printed work, and constituted an early form of copyright law.

The company's charter gave it the right to seize illicit editions and bar the publication of unlicensed books. The decree also stated that nothing could be reprinted without being re-licensed. The decree further stated that in all case the full signed imprimatur was to be printed; the names of the printer and the author were to be printed as well. The decree also limited the number of master printers to twenty, and specified the number of presses, journeymen and apprentices each could have. The decree also made it an offense to work for an unlicensed printer, or to operate an unlicensed press.[14]The genesis of copyright was thus the result of the anxiety of the crown to curb anything which is considered against its own interest's and to impose blatant censorship over the printed matters through the Stationer's company.[15]

4 SUPERVISION THROUGH STAR CHAMBER

The system of control was equally satisfying to Elizabeth and her Stuart successors, who supervised it through Star Chamber .By a later decree, by her, dated June 23, 1585, every book was required to be licensed and all persons were prohibited from printing any book, work, or copy against the form or meaning of any injunction made by Her Majesty or her Privy Councilor against the true intent and meaning of any letters patent commissions or prohibitions under the great seal or contrary to any allowed ordinance set down for the good government of the Stationers' Company.

In 1623, a proclamation was issued to enforce this decree reciting that it had been evaded amongst other ways by printing beyond the sea such allowed books, works or writings, as have been imprinted within the realm by such person to whom the sole printing authority thereof by letters patent or lawful ordinance or authority doth appertain.

In 1637, the Star Chamber codified its law on book licensing and printing and again decreed that:"no person is to print or import Of printed abroad) a book or copy which the Company of Stationers, or any person, hath or shall, by any letters patent, order or entrance in their register book, or otherwise, have the right, privilege, authority, or allowance, solely to print".

Until 1640, the Crown, using the Star Chamber as its instrument, rigorously enforced several decrees and ordinance of that Chamber regulating the manner of printing, the number of presses permitted to operate throughout the Kingdom, and prohibiting all printing against the force and meaning of any of the statutes or laws of the realm. This restrictive jurisdiction was enforced by the use of summary powers of search, confiscation and imprisonment, free of any obstruction from parliament.

5 END OF STATIONER'S COPYRIGHT

From 1557 to 1641, the English Crown exercised authority over printing and the Stationers' Company through the Star Chamber.

After the abolition of the Star Chamber in 1641, the English Parliament continued to extend the Stationers' Company's censorship/monopoly arrangement through a series of ordinances and Licensing Acts between 1643 and 1692. During its time, the Stationers' Company developed a private system for handling disputes between its members. Under this system, specific Guild members held monopoly rights in a particular work that were treated as being perpetual.[16]

Although Guild members could purchase a manuscript from an author, authors could not become members of the Guild and were not entitled to any royalties or additional payments after purchase. Members were allowed to buy and sell rights over particular works to each other. As a method to keep track of which members claimed rights in what works, the Guild required that copyrights be recorded in a registration book at the Guild's Hall.

6. FIRST LICENSING ACT

The Licensing Act of 1662 also required printers to deposit a copy of each work with the Guild to prevent changes to the work after it was reviewed by censors. Many aspects of the Stationers' system were later incorporated into modern copyright law.

It was an act for preventing the frequent abuses in printing seditious treasonable and unlicensed books and pamphlets and for regulating of printing and printing presses[17] which was passed in1662 and prohibited the printing of any book unless first licensed and entered in the register of the Stationers' Company.

The Act further prohibited any person from printing or importing, without the consent of the owner, any book which any person had the sole right to print by virtue of letters patent or by force or virtue of any entry or entries thereof duly made or to be made in the register book of the said Stationers' Company or in the register book of other universities.

The penalty for piracy was forfeiture of the books and six-shilling and eight pence for each copy of which half to go to the King and half to the owner. The sole property of the owner is here acknowledged in express terms as a common law right and so the legislature which passed that Act must have recognized the concept that the productions of the brain could be the subject-matter of property. To support an action on this statute the ownership of the book had to be proved or the plaintiff could not have recovered because the action was to be brought by the owner who was to have a half share of the penalty.

The various provisions of this Act in effect prevented piracy, without actions of law or Bills in equity. Cases of disputed property did, however, arise. Some of them were between different patentees of the Crown and in some the point was whether the property belonged to the author from his invention and labor, the King, from the subject matter. This was the first clear cut law which was aimed at protecting literally copyright and checking piracy. But, the license era was short lived .It expired in May, 1679.

7. STATUTE OF ANNE

The first copyright Act of 1709 gave the Stationer's the maximum of theoretical authority and the minimum of practical power. [18]It was only on 10thApril, 1710 that the law was passed and came into force. It was the first copyright law in the world and it is the foundation on which the modern concept of copyright was built[19]. The law was Queen's Anne Statute, after Queen Anne (known as "An Act for the encouragement of learning and securing the property of copies of books to the rightful owners thereof). In course of time, the bundle of author's exclusive rights has widened vastly, covering a variety of activities in respect of a variety of works. [20]The "sole right and liberty of printing books" that the Act conferred was given to authors and their assigns; but it seemed nonetheless from commercial exploitation rather than literary creation pure and simple.

According to its preamble, the Act responded to several objectives like the encouragement of learning, the prevention of the practice of piracy for the future and the encouragement of learned men to compose and write useful books.

The enforcement of the Statute of Anne in April of 1710 marked a historic moment in the development of copyright. The statute was concerned with the reading public, the continued production of useful literature, and the spread and advancement of education. The central plank of the statute is a social quid pro quo; to encourage "learned men to compose and write useful books". The statute guaranteed the finite right to print and reprint those works. It established a pragmatic bargain involving authors, the booksellers and public.[21]

It provided the authors for the first time, the statutory right to reprint their books, for a limited period of twenty-one years for works published before the date of enactment i.e.from10th April, 1710 those works which had not been transferred to stationer's Guild. Those works which were published subsequent to the enactment of Statute of Anne enjoyed a protection of fourteen years.

Prior to the Statute of Anne, the common law of England recognized a perpetual right of property in the author's "copy" in the manuscript.[22] The protection afforded was against the piracy of printed works. It did not include other creative works such as paintings, drawings, etc. which also by that time became targets of piracy, in addition to other aspects relating to piracy of books (translation, dramatization). Following this act, copyrighted works were required to be deposited at specific copyright libraries and registered at stationers Hall. There was no automatic protection for unpublished works.[23]

Penalties for infringement were stringent i. e. infringing books were subject to forfeiture and a fine of a penny for every sheet copied. This resulted in a steep fine when many copies of substantial work were pirated .It was only with the passing of the act, that the rights of the authors over their work came to be legally recognized and concept of "public domain "was established, though not explicitly. The statute was indeed a turning point in the history of copyright laws.[24]The Statute of Anne ended the old system whereby only literature that met the censorship standards administers by the booksellers could appear in print. It created a public domain for literature, as previously all literature belonged to the booksellers forever.[25]

In 1735, William Hogarth, after a lively public campaign, helped to pass an Act in the United Kingdom, giving engravers the rights to their work for fourteen years from publication. It was a landmark in the history of copyright as it bestowed on engravers similar legal rights to authors and stopped sellers of prints from creaming off all the profits .Later, the copyright has been extended in Britain to fifty years from the death of the author and on the Gower's report kept the existing limit of fifty years after death.[26]

Since1710, copyright has gradually increased its scope from book printing to include engraving, photography and film, sheet and recorded music, broadcasting and most recently, digital forms of communication and databases. With each new form of media, there was a step change in the culture of copyright. At the same time, as the number of media involved in copyright have increased the length of time, the duration that a work remains in copyright in the United Kingdom has increased very significantly from the original fourteen years set in1710 to forty-two in 1842,to fifty in1956,and then in1988,the current seventy years. Britain developed copyright as a property concept through the 18th and the 19th century, and still has the effort put into a work 'as part of its copyright value as well as the original 'creative value'.[27]

HISTORY OF COPYRIGHT LAW IN INDIA

In ancient India, knowledge has been spread through gurus and pundits by chanting shlokas orally. Later inscriptions were being made on leaves of trees i.e. talapatras. In India, kings used to patronize the authors i.e. literary scholars. Under the rule of East India Company, and British Crown, the procedure followed in Great Britain had been implemented in India regarding the Copyright protection of literary work. India, like most developing countries, received modern Copyright Law as a gift from its colonial rules.[28]

Modern Copyright law in India developed in India gradually, in a span of 150years.History and the development of copyright law in India closely parallels the history of British Copyright Laws as Administration in British occupied India was streamlined on English principles of justice, liberty and good conscience. The development of copyright law in India was gradual and based on British system.

The first ever copyright law that was applied in India was English Copyright Act, 1842.It was applied in the case of Macmillan v. Khan Bahadur Shamsul Ulama Zaka [29]even when this Act was not expressly applicable to India.[30]

The historicity of copyright law in India can be discussed under the following phases:

PHASE 1: THE COPYRIGHT ACT, 1847:

The law relating to Copyright begins in India when East India Company extended the English Copyright Act of 1847 to the territories under its control.[31]The Act was passed by the Governor General of India and was enacted on 8th December, 1847 much earlier than many other countries. It's preamble recites several doubts which exist or which" may exist" concerning recognition and enforcement of copyright as a part of the common law or administration of justice on the basis of justice, equity and good conscience" or as regards the application of British statutes to territories then administered by the East India Company.

The Act focuses on books, and the right to copy (as opposed to the expanded spectrum of works and rights contemporary copyright contemplates).[32]

According to the enactment of 1847, the term of Copyright was the natural life of the author and seven years post mortem auctoris (PMA) and in no case, it was to exceed the period of forty-two years.[33]The government was having the power to grant a license (compulsory) to publish a book if the Copyright owner, upon author's death refused to allow its publication.[34]If any person in an unauthorized manner i.e. without the consent of the proprietor was involved in the sale hire, exportation, selling, publishing of the copyright work, then the suit or action for infringement was to be filed in the highest local court having original civil jurisdiction.[35]

Section 10 of the Act specifically provides that under a contract of service, copyright in any review, encyclopedia, magazine, periodical work or work published in a series of books or parts shall vest in the proprietor, projector, publisher or conductor. Infringing copies were deemed to be the copies of proprietor of copyrighted work .Importantly, unlike today; copyright in a work was not automatic.

Registration of copyright with the Home Office was compulsory under the Act for the right's enforcement but it was explicitly stated that that the non- registration of copyright would not affect the subsistence of the Copyright .Further ,the non-registration of copyright only denied copyright owners the right to maintain a suit under the provisions of the1847Indian Copyright Act-the statute itself explicitly stated that owners of unregistered Copyrights had 'the right to sue or proceed in respect of the infringement thereof, under the provisions of the Act.

At the time of its introduction in India, Copyright law had already been in the developing stage in Britain for over a century and hence, the provisions of the 1847 enactment in India were reflected in the later enactments.[36] Copyright law in its modern sense, was both abstract (encompassing 'all works 'of literature and art) and forward looking in the way that it sought to accommodate both existing and new forms of subject matter. This enactment created the conceptual milieu that eased the passage of succeeding legislations. This statute continued till 1911.

An interesting feature of British, this phase of copyright protection in the country is that while in Britain ,the university of Cambridge and Oxford ,the four Universities in Scotland, and the several colleges of Eton, Westminster as well Trinity college, Dubbling, had the right to 'hold in perpetuity their copyright in books given or bequeathed to them for the advancement of useful learning and other purposes of education', whereas, Universities in India such as Kolkata, Mumbai and Chennai did not have such a right.[37]

PHASE 2: THE COPYRIGHT ACT, 1914

The Indian Copyright Act, 1914 which was the first modern copyright legislation in India was incorporated from the Imperial Copyright Act; 1911.Two major changes were made under the Act. First of all, it introduced criminal sanctions for copyright Infringement under sections7-12. Secondly, it modified the scope of the term of copyright; under section4 the "sole right" of the author to" produce, reproduce, perform or publish a translation of a work shall subsist only for a period of ten years from the date of first publication of the work."

The author, however retained his/her sole rights if within the period of ten years, he published or authorized publication of his work or translation in any language in respect of that language. The modification of term of copyright for translation rights had adverse impact and disadvantageous to the authors and a boon to publishers. This Act has been elaborated by judicial decisions like *Macmillan v. R.C. Cooper*[38] vesting violations or property rights with criminal sanctions can probably be understood as a part of general colonial legal and political policies which sought to protect the right to property over rights to personal freedom.

The modification of term of copyright for translation rights however cannot be explained by any reference to dominant characteristics of colonial policy. The language of the Act might suggest a laudable policy objective of promoting wider diffusion of Indian works in one language into other Indian languages, a consideration which might have appeared distinctive to India as compared with UK.

There might also have been the desire to promote the growth of publication industry in numerous Indian languages. But whatever be the intention, the impact was disadvantageous to the authors and a boon to publishers. This can be seen from the following observations in a note of dissent when the continuation of the same provision was urged by the Joint Select Committee of the Indian Parliament in 1956 (a recommendation which did not ultimately prevail). Ram Dhari Singh Dinkar (renowned Hindi poet designated as national poet for his contribution to national literature) argued that this provision has worked to the utter detriment of the authors.

Referring to the plight of two distinguished Bengali authors, he observed: "Most of the novels by Sarat Chandra Chatterjee were translated in Hindi, while the author was yet alive. The author's novels, in translation sold thousands of copies, but the author did not get a pie out of the sale proceeds. Publishers in Hindi and other languages were making good money out of the translations of his works, but the poets were getting nothing.

Mostly, the publishers in Hindi language were making a huge amount of profits from the modification of the Copyright's term regarding translations .Hindi was emerging as a dominant language in Northern India. The early phases of the law produced decisions like *Macmillan v. Suresh Chander Deb*[39]and *Macmillan v. R.C cooper*[40]which have become locus classicus of the copyright law. It generated a juristic dependencia. Indian judicial decisions as well as forensic styles have had perforce to rely on UK precedents.

There was a heavy hand of UK law on Indian creative works. Judicial interpretation was influenced by the law of UK. The slavish imitation of foreign precedents has occasionally led intrepid Indian justices to remind the Bar and the Bench that the 1957 Act is made by 'a sovereign legislature of this land' and its interpretation 'must be based upon the object of the legislation and the language used' and that the 'historical roots' of the Indian law in the UK law of copyright should have no higher function than that of providing an aid to thinking. The 1914Act remained applicable in India force until it was replaced by the Copyright Act, 1957.[41]

PHASE 3: INDIAN COPYRIGHT ACT, 1957

The creative intelligence of man is displayed in multiform ways of aesthetic expression but it often happens that the economic system so operates that the priceless divinity which is called artistic or literary creativity in man is exploited and masters, whose works are invaluable are victims of piffling payments. World opinion in defense of human right to intellectual property led to international conventions and municipal laws, commissions, codes and organization, calculated to protect works of art. India responded to this universal need by enacting the Copyright Act, 1957.

This is how Krishna Iyer J described the object of the Indian Copyright Act, 1957 in the case of *Indian Performing Rights Society Ltd. v Eastern India Motion Pictures Association.*[42]

This Act was passed in the seventh year of republic as there was a dire need of own copyright law. It was brought into force on 24th January, 1958. There were tremendous reasons for the passing of the Act. Firstly, it was very clear that continued existence of the 1911 Act through the 1914Act was unbecoming to 'the changed constitutional status of India.' Secondly, the 1914 Act was not in accordance with the 1948 Brussels Act of the Berne Convention and the 1952 Universal Copyright Convention- chiefly in the much longer terms that the Berne Convention mandated.

Thirdly, during the five decades, modern and advanced means of communications like broadcasting, litho-photography, television etc have made roads in Indian economy and rendered modernization of the law as necessary. Fourthly, the need for an 'independent self-contained law' was also felt in the light of the experience of the 'working' of the 1911 Act, and more importantly, the growing public consciousness of the rights and obligations of the authors was another factor which mandated the passing of the Act.[43]Moreover, the advancement in the technique of reprography, audio-visual technologies and exponential growth of personal computers also led to the passing of the Act.

After considering the reports of English copyright committee, Select committee and Indian organizations and legislative proposals based thereon, the copyright Act, 1957 was made. The Act was in no way a replication of the English legislative proposals. It was a true Indian legislation made by its independent legislature .This was a roadmap to the modern Copyright law.

The general scheme and the principal features of the act are as follows. The Act was divided into 15chapters and 79 sections. Chapters I, III, IV and V deals with copyright and its ownership; chapter VIII with the rights of broadcasting authorities, chapter IX deals with international copyright, Chapter X with registration of copyright, chapter XI deals with infringement ,chapter XII-XIV with civil and criminal remedies and chapters II ,VI,VII,X with powers and functions of the registrar of copyrights and Copyright Board.

Copyright rules were enacted under serction78.They deal with matters of procedure primarily in matters mainly like applications of licenses for translations, performing rights societies, relinquishment and registration of copyright and related matters. Moreover, the government is empowered to make an order directing that any or all the provisions of the act may apply to copyright in foreign works of certain international organizations. The orders are to be laid before Parliament and subject to modifications by it. The orders have to be published in the official gazette.

This Act also recognized administrative setup for implementation and protection of copyright in India. It creates two distinct institutions: the Copyright Office and the Copyright Board. The Copyright Office is headed by a registrar of copyrights and the office is under the direction and superintendence of the Indian Government. The Ministry of Education and Social Welfare is the administrative body regulating and controlling the Copyright Office. Copyright Board has been given the appellate status.

The Act has been amended five times i.e. 1983, 1984, 1992, and 1999 and most recently in 2012.

1983 AMENDMENT

In 1983, provisions have been made for copyright in lectures, address etc. delivered in public and for copyright in lectures, address etc.[44] Sections 32A and 32B provided for` compulsory licenses' for publication of copyrighted foreign works in any Indian language for the purposes of systematic instructional activities at a `low price‘ with the permission of the Copyright Board on certain conditions. The other crucial change was the insertion of section 19A, relating to the conferral of power in the Copyright Board, upon a due complaint to it, to order revocation of the assigned copyright where either the terms are 'harsh‘ or where the publication of the work is unduly delayed.

In addition, the 1983Amendment provides for power in the Copyright Board to publish unpublished Indian works, and for the protection of 'oral works‘. The amendment made it mandatory for the copyright office to publish details of all copyright registrations in the Gazette of India. Lastly, they disallowed the importation of an 'infringing copy‘ of a copyright work for 'private and domestic use' which had been permissible prior to the amendment.[45]

1984 AMENDMENT

The 1984 amendment, following the wake of vociferous concern about the piracy of copyrighted works, provides for strict punishments for piracy and effective procedures to inhibit it. This amendment was related to the inclusion of video film, provided protection of computer programs, empowered police to search without warrant, enhanced punishment and declared copyright infringement and related rights as an economic offence etc.

1992 AMENDMENT

The term of the copyright protection was extended for a period of ten years which raised the term of copyright protection and total period of copyright become life plus 60years in general.

1994 AMENDMENT

It's considered as an important amendment to the Indian Copyright Act,1957.This amendment changes the definition of the term 'adaptation' and 'author 'in terms of cinematograph, copyright board and its powers were reconstituted, changes were made in the rights of copyright owner, assignments and licenses which brought' copyright societies in place of performing rights societies, introduction of author's special rights, changes were made in offences relating to use of infringing copy of a computer program and rule making powers of the government were also changed. The main motive behind this amendment was to bring it in consonance with the TRIPS agreement.

It extended more effectively protection to owners of copyright and related rights in the context of technological developments affecting the reproduction of works by, inter alia , bringing within the scope of copyright the subsequent hire or sale of copies of cinematograph films, computer programmes and sound recordings.[46]

1999 AMENDMENT

The amendment was associated with sections38,40A,42Aand52etc.Under this Act, the duration of the performer's rights were extended to fifty years .Second important amendment was the power of the central government to apply chapter-VIII of the Act to the broadcasting organizations and performers in certain other countries on the same platform, if it appears to the central government that a foreign country does not give or has not undertaken to give adequate protection to rights of broadcasting organizations or performers, the Central Government, by order published in the official gazette, direct that such of the provisions of the Act shall not apply to performers or broadcasting organizations. The amendment was an attempt to enforce the treaty obligations by honoring its international commitments in furtherance of Article 253 of the Constitution of India.

2012 AMENDMENT

The Copyright (Amendment) Act2012 came into effect from June 21, 2012. These amendments have made the copyright Act, more in line with WIPO treaties, besides incorporating issues relating to digital storage and digital transmission of copyrighted material.[47] It, in many ways revolutionized the Copyright laws in India and has made certain changes with regard to laws against piracy. It extended the performer's and broadcasting organization's rights, the major thrust of it was on eliminating unequal treatment meted out to lyricists and music composers of copyrighted works incorporated in cinematograph film owing to the contractual practice in the entertainment industry of India. Lyricist and music composers after assigning all rights for a one time-lump sum payment were having no further right to any royalty accruing from their work even if the work was being utilized in mediums other than the cinematograph film. Hence a proviso was added to section17, which provided that clauses (b) and(c) of the section will have no effect on the author of the work.

Further, it broadened the scope of statutory and compulsory licensing provisions and empowered the broadcasting organizations to broadcast any prior published literary, musical work and sound recording by giving a prior notice to the copyright owner and paying royalty at the rates prescribed by the Copyright Board.[48]Section52(1)(z b)was inserted which allowed the conversion of any work in any accessible format by any person or organization till such reproduction is for the benefit of persons with any disability and the converting organization is working on a non-profit basis.

It introduced sections65Aand65B to promote Digital Rights Management and to protect the rights of copyright owners in digital domain. The new section 65A protects the technological protection measures (TPM) used by copyright owners against circumvention. TPM is used by a copyright owner to protect his rights on the work. In case, a person circumvents it with the intention of infringing such rights, then that person would be punishable with imprisonment up to 2years and shall also be liable for fine.

Section 65B of the Act makes removal of right management information without authority and distribution thereafter a criminal offence. Information rights Management (IRM) is a term that applies to a technology which protects sensitive information from unauthorized access. So, any unauthorized and intentional removal or alteration of any rights management information is a criminal offence punishable with imprisonment. The introduction of Sections 65A and 65B is to help the film, music and publishing industry in fighting piracy.[49]

Further, to ensure that the digital advances are useful for the users and do not restrict access unreasonably and to protect the Internet service providers in section52 (b) and52(c) are inserted. These provisions protect ISPs from liability of copyright infringement in case of transient and incidental storage of the work for the purpose of providing access.[50]

CONCLUSION

The Copyright law has travelled a long journey since the invention of the printing press by Guttenberg to the Indian Copyright Act, 1957. This long journey has seen many developments such as the advancement in communication and technology which has further made the distribution of work very easy within a few time. That's the only reason that the Act has been amended from time to time to bring it in consonance with the present needs of the society. Moreover, the amendments have been made in accordance with the legal system and practices followed under the Indian Constitution. A few years ago, the knowledge about copyright was less and people were aware about the piracy of literary works including books, but with the passage of time and continuous development of the society, it's becoming aware of the different forms of copyright infringement and the need to protect the creative works in any form, format and media which is the need of the hour.

[1] Peterson J in University of London vs. University of Tutorial Process Ltd. 1916(2)Ch 601

[2] C.S. Lal, Intellectual Property Handbook, Law Publishers India Pvt. Limited, Allahabad, 2005,p.19

[3] 1984AIR 667

[4] < http://www.lawyersclubindia.com> retrieved on 12thAugust,2016

[5] Charu Dureja, 'Historical Development Of C opyright Law in India' ,International Journal of Advanced Research in Management and Social Sciences, Volume 4, No.1,(2015), p.51

[6] Darrell L. Peck, Copyright-Infringement Of Literary Works-An Elemental Analysis, Marquette Law Review, Volume 38 Issue 3 Winter 1954-1955,p.180

[7] John Gantz, and Jack B. Rochester, Pirates of the Digital Medium, Upper Saddle River: Financial Times Prentice Hall, NJ,205,p. 30-33

[8] A Subbian, "Intellectual Property Rights" ,Deep and Deep Publications Pvt. Ltd., New Delhi,p.287

[9] S R Saha, 'Management of Intellectual Property Rights ,Indian Law Institute, New Delhi, p.6

[10] Javed Siddiqui, Intellectual Property Rights-Legal Perspective, Cyber Tech Publications, New Delhi ,First Edition,2012, p.84

[11] J.A.L Sterling, World Copyright Law, 3rd edn., London, Sweet and Maxwell, 2008, p.8

[12] W.R.Cornish, Intellectual Property: Patents, Copyright, Trademarks and Allied Rights, Universal Law Publishing Co. Pvt. Ltd., Delhi, Third Edition,p.297

[13] Jaqueline M.B. Seignette, Challenges to the creator Doctrine-Authorship, Copyright Ownership and the Exploitation of Creative Works in the Netherlands, Germany and the United States, 1994,p.13

[14] <www.historyofinformation.com/expanded.php?id=3899> retrieved on 2nd August,2016

[15] Avinash Shinde, Intellectual Property Manual, Lexis Nexis Butterworks, Edition 2004,p.20

[16] Rajendra Raghav, Cyber Law and Intellectual Property Rights, Cyber Tech Publications, New Delhi, p.53

[17]< http://historyand18cnovel.tumblr.com/post/534952351/the-1662-licensing-of-the-press-act> retrieved on 21st August,2016

[18] <http://copyright-debate.co.uk/?p=184> retrieved on 2nd August,2016

[19] G.Davis, Copyright and the Public Interest, 2nd Edition, Sweet and Maxwell, 2002,p.11

[20] Jagdish Sagar, Zakir Thomas, Raman Mittal, Copyright, faculty of Law, year...,P.2

[21] Ronan, Deazley, 'Rethinking copyright: history, theory, language, Edward Elgar Publishing Co.,p.13-14

[22] Akhil Prasad and Aditi Aggarwala, 'Common Law Copyright', Copyright Law Desk Book,2009,p.127

[23]<http://www.iprightsoffice.org/copyright_history/> retrieved on 2nd August,2016

[24] Id. ,p.132-133

[25] Edward Samuels,' The Public Domain in Copyright Law',41 Journal of the Copyright Society 137(1993) retrieved at <http://www.edwardsamuels.com/copyright/beynd/articles/public.html#fn25>at 25thSeptember,2016

[26] Dr. S.R. Myneni, "Law of Intellectual Property ",Asia Law House, Hyderabad,7th Edition,2014,p.45

[27]< http://copyrightsandwrongs.nen.gov.uk/ipr-and-copyright/history_of_copyright> retrieved on 31st July,2016

[28] Dr. Mira T. Sundarajan, Digital Learning in India: Problems and prospects, retrieved at <http://www.cyber.law.harvard.education/home/dl_india>

[29](1895)I.L.R Bom.557

[30] R. Madhawan v. S.K. Nayer, AIR 1988Ker 39(45)

[31] Baxi, Upendra,' Copyright Law and Justice in India', Journal of Indian Law Institute,1986,p.497

[32]< http://copyright.lawmatters.in/2014/04/indias-first-1847-copyright-statute.html?m=1> retrieved on 1st August,2016

[33] Section 1 of The Copyright Act,1847

[34] Section 2of The Copyright Act,1847

[35] Section 7 of The Copyright Act,1847

[36] Rajkumar S.Adukia, *Handbook on Intellectual Property Rights in India,* http://www.metastudio.org/Science%20and%20Ethics/file/readDoc/535a76367d9d331598f49e2d/34_Hb_on_IPR.pdf, accessed on 26-08-2016 at 10-11.

[37] James, T.C., Copyright Law of India and the Academic Community, Vol .IX, JIPR, May 2004,p.12

[38] AIR1924PC75

[39] (1890)ILR 17Cal 951

[40] (1924)26BOMLR292

[41] V.K Ahuja, Law of Copyright and Neighboring Rights: National and International Perspectives,2007,p.2-3

[42] 1977AIR 1443, 1977SCR(3)206

[43] Statement of objects and reasons to the Report of Joint Select Committee

[44] The Object of the Copyright(Amendment) Act,1983

[45]< http://nostalgicmans.blogspot.in/2009/01/history-of-copyright-in-india.html?m=1> retrieved on 31st July,2016

[46] D.P.Mittal, Law Relating To Copyright, Patent & Trade Mark And GATT, Taxmann Allied Services(P) Ltd., New

Delhi,1994, p.468

[47] Neeraj Pandey and Khushdeep Dharni, Intellectual Property Rights, PHI learning Private Limited, Delhi, Edition 2014,p.63

[48] Section 31D,Copyright Act,1957

[49] <http://spicyip.com/2013/01/guest-post-taking-look-at-online-piracy.html> retrieved on 6th September,2016

[50] Abhai Pandey, Inside Views: The Indian Copyright(Amendment)Act,2012 and its functioning so far, at <http://www.ip-watch.org/2014/10/23/the-indian-copyright-amendment-act-2012-and-its-functioning-so-far/> retrieved on 21/08/2016

CHAPTER XII

LAWS AND PRACTICES RELATING TO F.I.R. IN INDIA {Author: Vipul R. R. Malhotra}

Meaning and Purpose of Study-

To conduct a detailed study on the subject as well as practical aspect of First Information Report under the ambits of Indian Criminal Laws, prima facie one must know and there is a need to introduce that What is law, What is practice, What is First Information Report.[1] This is so because one can only conduct a complete and well satisfied research on the subject, over which he/ she has a satisfactorily knowledge and furthermore, it is to be taken into consideration that the research which is to be carried, must be bona-fide for the people contributing to the society at large. Hence, by providing an answer to the above-mentioned questions we may conclude that law is a very wide field. It has a transitional character. Law changes with the passage of time, place, era and evolution and because of this transitional aspect of law, each and every thinker, scholar, jurist or expert has given different view point on the subject of law. Thus, because of various definitions present on the subject of law, it is very difficult to define that what actually law is. Because at some places what actually law is, may or may not be considered as law at another place. Howsoever, it is essential to understand as per layman's language that what law is & the following diagrammatical set up will help us to understand that what actually law includes and what it does not include- • Hence, law includes-

1. The set of rules.
2. Regulations to reduce criminal acts.
3. Ways to impart justice.

Furthermore, there is a need to study the purpose of studying the law. As we had already discussed that law is set of rules and regulations used to provide justice in civil as well as criminal matters. The abovementioned definition clearly shows the significance of studying the practical aspects of law. Furthermore, the following elements from the word LAW will help us to define the purpose of law in detail-

- FORMULAE TO UNDERSTAND PURPOSE OF LAW-
- L- Legal
- A- Aspects To Control
- W- World
- LEGAL+ASPECTS+(OF) WORLD=LAW
- NOTE- It is to be kept in mind that the above-mentioned formulae is the self-created formulae of the researcher for to simplify the subject of understanding the purpose of the field of law for the generations to come.

Relevance of Practice in the field of Law-

Further-more the research states that what actually the term practice refers to. Though it is a very general term but it is important to define this term because it is included in the title of our research study and a good researcher must ascertain the depth of its research study. Normally, practice is defined as the process of performing an action again & again to get perfection. But while studying the concept of practice in detail, the researcher has come to know that it plays a vital role, not only in the field of law but almost in each & every sphere of life & in each and every field of study. Now let us discuss the relevance of the concept of practice in the field of law3 . But in order to discuss the relevance of practice in the field of law, one must know that what is the difference between a lawyer and an advocate. By providing an answer to the abovementioned question one may conclude the following analysis-

- **Lawyer**-A person who studies law.

- **Advocate**-A person who practices law.
- **Lawyer**-A lawyer may or may not be an Advocate.
- **Advocate**-An Advocate is always a lawyer.
- **Lawyer**-Example- A student of a law.
- **Advocate**-Example- An Advocate of court of School. Law such as Sir Kapil Sibbal.

From above explanations, it is very much clear & specific that practice is the subject which helps in bringing perfection to each & every field and it is only because of the result of practice which helps to analyse the principle of legal aspect which says that, "A good lawyer must know something about everything and everything about something."

Meaning of F.I.R. in detail-

Now after discussing both the abovementioned subjects of law & practice in detail, there is a need to study that What First Information Report actually is. This is so because in order to conduct a detailed-research on the concept of Law[2]& Practices regarding F.I.R. in India, one must know the depth of law, practice and F.I.R. as well. By providing an answer to the abovementioned question the researcher may conclude that in case of non-bailable offence, the written report which is being drafted by the Police officials on behalf of the receival of Prima facie information regarding the commission of such & such non-bailable offence is termed as First Information Report as well. It is not always compulsory that such & such F.I.R. (being explained above) is to be introduced by victim of such non-bailable offence but instead it can be lodged by any other person on behalf of victim as well.

Procedure to register F.I.R. in India-

In context to this the utmost important subject of discussion is that, that what is the actual procedure to record the F.I.R. as per the ambits of Indian laws. By providing specific information to this questionnaire, the researcher wants to attract the attention towards Sec. 154 of Cr.P.C[3]. (of 1973) which includes the following essential pointers to describe the abovementioned aspect- When

Police receives the information regarding the happening of a non-bailable offence in an oral format, then the Police is obliged to write it down. The authority is given to a person giving information regarding the commission of a non-bailable offence to demand that the information being recorded by the Police is read over to this person being informant of the incident. Thereafter, this recorded information is to be signed by the informant of the entire incident as well. But Prima facie, it is to be kept in mind by the informant of above mentioned non-bailable incident that he/she should sign the report recorded by the Police as a form of FIR only by verifying the details given by him/her. Now furthermore, it is also the right of the informant to ask for the copy of FIR, if the Police refuses to give it to the informant. Furthermore, it is also to be kept in mind that such & such copy of FIR is to be provided free of cost by the Police to the person giving information of the incident as well. In context to this the question arises that if any person giving information of the non-bailable offence to the Police officials is illiterate and is unable to perform signatures then what alternative is there under the legal ambits to resolve this issue. By providing an answer to the abovementioned aspect the doctrinal study of the researcher may conclude that such & such illiterate persons have the right to put their left thumb impression on such a document of F.I.R. after being verifying that it is a right and perfect record as well.

Alternatives available if Police refuses to register F.I.R.-

In context to this the question arises that if Police officials refuses to register the F.I.R. then what alternatives are constitutionally available to the person who want to register the F.I.R.[4]. as well. In order to answer the abovementioned issue, the following alternatives are available under the legal ambits of Indian criminal lawsOne has the right to consult the Superintendent of Police or other higher officers like Deputy Inspector General of Police or Police & Inspector General of Police and bring the complaint to their notice. Thereafter, one has the right to send the complaint in writing & by post to the Superintendent of Police associated. If the Superintendent of Police deems fit, then he shall either investigate the complaint himself/herself or order its subordinates to conduct the investigation. Furthermore, one has the right to file a private complaint before the court having jurisdiction. Finally, one has the right to make a complaint to the SHRC or the NHRC if the Police does nothing to enforce the law or does it in a corrupt & biased manner.

F.I.R. - A Backbone to administer criminal justice-

It is not wrong, to say that F.I.R. is a backbone for providing justice with respect to criminal and non-bailable matters involved. This is so because it brings the process of justice in motion. Furthermore, F.I.R. plays a vital role for to investigate the case and SHO is the Police official who is obliged to conduct such & such investigation as well. Furthermore, the SHO is obliged to keep the 11 W's in mind while investigating the matter associated with the aspect of F.I.R. as well and these 11 W's are listed as follows[5]-

1. W- When the offence has been committed.
2. W-Where it has been committed.
3. W-Why (Motive of commission).
4. W-What information has come to convey.
5. W-What capacity.
6. W-Who committed crime.
7. W-Whom against crime is committed.
8. W-Which may (actual occurrence).
9. W-Witnesses.
10. W-What was taken away.
11. W-What traces were left by the accused.

F.I.R.- As a foundation to administer justice under criminal laws-

Though F.I.R. is not defined clearly under Cr.P.C. but yet it is the foundation to administer justice with respect to criminal matters. The relevance of F.I.R. has been explained in the matter of State of Haryana vs. Bhajan Lal15. As per the judgement of this case F.I.R. is a very valuable document. It is very essential document not only for prosecution but for the defence also. As we had explained earlier that F.I.R. is a foundation for the entire case and if, the foundation will be weak then the case of prosecution would be in worse situation and if it would be strong then it has the strength to tackle the attacks of accused and his counsel. This clearly shows that F.I.R. is directly proportional to the case of prosecution as well. The following formulae completely explains the abovementioned para-

F.I.R. Effects on the case of prosecution.

In context to this the question arises in front of a layman that who has the authority to write the F.I.R. Many people are confused with regard to this matter that whether every Police official has the authority to record the F.I.R. or not. By providing an answer to this question the researcher concludes that only the officer in charge of the Police Station has the authority to record the F.I.R, popularly known as SHO. Howsoever by paying attention towards Sec. 36 of Cr.P.C. the researcher may further concludes that the superior or senior officer of the officer in charge of the Police Station has also the proper authority to record such & such F.I.R. in case of non-bailable offences as well. Now it is very much clear that F.I.R. is recorded for heinous offences and sometimes, it is very much difficult for the informer of the happening of non-bailable offence to reach the officer in charge of the Police Station and thus, now the question arises that whether the information of happening of such &such non-bailableoffence, if given to the Police constable is valid or not. By providing an answer to the abovementioned issue the doctrinal research of the researcher wants to attract the attention towards sec. 157 of the Indian Evidence Act (of 1872) which says that it is also valid to give information of the concerned incident to any of the Police official (including the Police constables) and furthermore, it is the obligation of such constable or any other Police official to give information of the receival of such complaint to the officer in charge of the Police Station, so that he/she must note down the F.I.R. regarding the same.

Procedure available to delay the lodging of F.I.R.-

In context to this one more question arises in front of researchers, layman etc.; that whether there is a provision to delay the lodging of F.I.R. under the statutory ambits of India or not. By referring to the abovementioned issue the researcher concludes that if possible, then one must not delay the lodging of F.I.R. This is so because it will act as a bane for prosecution in future. Howsoever, in certain reasonable circumstances one has the right to delay the F.I.R. but these circumstances are rare and let us discuss the following circumstances during which one has the right to delay the F.I.R. as well- Reasons for delaying can be-

- In case of worse psychological condition of the informer.
- In case of worse physical condition of the informer.
- In case of any natural calamity.
- In case of distance of place of occurrence from the Police Station.
- In case of late detection of commission of crime.
- Because of reasonable social & economic issues.
- Because of the dispute over the jurisdiction of Police Station.
- Because of un-avoidable departmental formalities (including delay due to opinion of experts).
- Because of threat, promise and undue influence.

Because of un-certainity of place of occurrence due to continuous offence.

- Because of shortage of staff associated with Police department.
- Because of the ignorance of the informer by the Police department.
- In context to this we have successfully discussed all the reasons which can be given by the informer of the non-bailable offence in case of delay for lodging the F.I.R. but in order to apply any of the abovementioned reason, there must be a reasonable ground for this delayand prima facie, one has to mention this reason in a well-satisfied manner during the lodging of its F.I.R.[6] and it

is to be mentioned within the F.I.R. as well.

4. **Empirical survey conducted in the forms of question/ answers at Police Station of Himachal Pradesh (INDIA) to understand the subject of F.I.R.-**

- **Q.No. 1-**
- What is the effect of F.I.R. on govt. jobs?
- **Answer by SHO-**
- Yes, many a times it has been found that most of the layman remains confused regarding the issue that what will happen, if F.I.R. has been registered against the govt. employee. By providing an answer to the abovementioned issue, we will conclude that simply the registeration of F.I.R. against the govt. employee will not snatch the job of such & such employee. Howsoever, if F.I.R. has been registered against him/her then he/she might be immediately suspended from his/her job, so that he/she cannot use his/her post for undue & illegal advantage. Howsoever, it is to be kept in mind that this suspension is not permanent in nature and will only continue till the completion of the criminal trial and once, it is proved in the court of law that the govt. employee against whom such & such F.I.R. has been registered, is innocent and is not guilty of the case being registered against him/her, then he/she has the right to resume and join his/her job as well. But if, on the other hand, it is proved that such & such govt. employee against whom such F.I.R. has been registered is guilty of such non-bailable offence then he/she is permanently debarred from his/ her job and a permanent expulsion is introduced against him/ her by the particular, govt. under whose jurisdiction his/her job lies as well. Now further-more it is also to be kept in mind that if the honourable District court convicts any govt. employee for the commission of non-bailable offence and he/she files appeal against this judgement in the honourable High Court then again, he/she will not permanently be expelled out from his/her job

until or unless the honourable High Court would deliver its judgement against such an employee and if the govt. employee again files the appeal against the orders of hon'ble High Court, in the honourable Supreme court of India, then again he/she would not be permanently expelled out from his/her job until the judgement of Supreme Court comes against him/her and if, the Supreme court gives judgement in favour of such a person then he/she has the right to join its job again as stated above.

- **Q.No.- 02-**
- What is Zero F.I.R.? Why Police sometimes refuses to register Zero F.I.R.?
- **Answer by SHO-**
- We all know that F.I.R. is usually registered in case of urgent non-bailable commissions and as a result of it, sometimes it is very difficult for the informer of the non-bailable commission to reach the Police Station which has the jurisdiction to try that offence because of certain reasons of fear, threat perception etc., and as a result of which the subject of Zero F.I.R. has been introduced within the legal ambits of criminal law structure which means that a person or usually the victim has the right to inform any of the Police Station which is actually nearest to the spot of the commission of a non-bailable offence as well. Now further-more the question arises in the mind of a layman that what is the significance of Zero F.I.R. By providing an answer to this issue one can conclude that zero F.I.R. is very much significant to begin the process of administering justice to the victim of non-bailable offence because once the zero F.I.R. is registered at a particular Police Station in front of an officer in charge of that Police Station (no matter whether the criteria to register such & such F.I.R. lies within the jurisdiction of that Police Station or not) then it is the obligation & is the formal duty of that Police Station to send the intimation of the record of such zero F.I.R. to the Police Station within whose jurisdiction the matter lies actually. Further-more by providing answer to the second question of the researcher, the officer in charge of the

Police Station at Jawalamukhi, District Kangra, H.P. has replied that it is totally wrong to conclude that the Police department refuses to register zero F.I.R. This is so because not even in the state of H.P. but instead in the entire nation, the Police department never refuses to register zero F.I.R. as well. One of the best example, of zero F.I.R. includes the commission of a heinous non-bailable offence by Asha Ram Bapu. In this landmark case, the zero F.I.R. was registered, prima facie, by the Delhi Police and the record of such registeration was sent to Rajasthan Police because the case actuallylies within the jurisdictional ambits of the territory of Rajasthan as well and look at the result of this effective zero F.I.R. because of which Asha RamBapu is behind the bars today. So, from the abovementioned example we may conclude that the subject of zero F.I.R. has enhanced the efficiency of criminal laws in India and the Police department is continuously working in favour of the victim regarding the registry of zero F.I.R. as well.

5. **F.I.R.- Whether Substantive piece of evidence under criminal laws-**

An FIR[7] is not a substantive piece of evidence. That is, it cannot be considered as evidence of facts stated therein. However, FIR may be used for the following purposes:

1. It can be used to corroborate an informant witness u/s 157 of Evidence Act. But it cannot be used to contradict or discredit other witnesses.
2. It can be used to contradict an informant witness u/s 145 of Evidence Act.
3. FIR can be used by the defence to impeach the credit of the maker under sec. 155(3) of the Evidence Act.
4. A non-confessional FIR given by an accused can be used as an admission against him u/s 21 of Evidence Act[8].

Statement of research problem-

The present research is triggered to tackle and answer large number of questions and debates about the challenges faced by lay-man while registering FIRs in India regarding the commission of cognizable offences. The study will not only throw light on these challenges, but it is also providing solutions to these lay-mans to curb these problems as well. The major questions which present research work is going to answer includes the following-

1. What is the effect of F.I.R. on govt. jobs?
2. What is Zero F.I.R.? Why Police sometimes refuses to register Zero F.I.R.?

Significance & Purpose-

The research study attempts to develop a report leading to identify the concept of FIR as a discipline under criminal laws. The research further attempts to study the drawbacks associated with registering of FIR in India. It further ensures the ways to overcome these challenges or drawbacks by providing the satisfactorily ways to modify & to refine the functioning of the Police department and by transforming the complex structure of Indian judicial system into simple one, plus to train the police officers with the complex procedural aspects of Indian judiciary. Furthermore, the study provides answer to the question that why there is a need to guide Police officials with regard to complex criminal laws of Indian ambits as well.Howsoever, the following objectives have been designed for the present study

- To identify and explore the development of the concept of First Information Report with the passage of time, place and era.
- To study the challenges faced by Police because of complex structure of Indian laws.
- To study & critically analyse the role of judiciary with the help of decided case laws.
- To study the significance of FIR to supress crime in India.

Literature review-

It is very essential to study the subject of F.I.R. especially in the State like India because it brings the process of administering criminal justice in motion. Howsoever, many common people face a lot of problem before lodging F.I.R. because of complex structure of Indian laws and sometimes because of lack of knowledge of certain Police officials. This problem is reflected in several statutory provisions, in large number of documents, books, articles, newspapers, magazines, websites etc...It would be very appropriate to make a brief review of some important books, articles and websites relating to this problem-

1. The twenty second edition of the Book, " The Code of Criminal Procedure" is a comprehensive one, written by Prof. S.N. Mishra. It at large provides the commentary on case laws right from 1950 to 2021. It also complies the relevant particulars relating to reports of the law commission, Parliament standing committee report and the repealed provisions on the subject, which is going to be very resourceful to have full insight on the topic and even evaluate the reasons of evolution as well as necessity of amendments made from time to time by legislature.
2. Book, The Indian Penal Code, by Prof. S.N. Mishra helped the researcher to explain the meaning of law and criminal law11 . The author has segregated the complete Act in twenty-three chapters on the line of structure as provided in the Act itself and further with each section has given an explanatory commentary in respect of various terms used in the provisions/sections. They are on regular basis supported by various decisions and authorities to enhance deep understanding of the same. In addition to it, the most resourceful section of the book in respect of the present work shall be the extracts of the relevant portion of the reports provided by the author. Hence it can be stated that it is very difficult to study the subject of FIR without the two essential elements of criminal laws which includes The IPC, which is a substantive law and The CrPC which is a procedural

law and forms the due process of law as well.

3. There are certain other books, the reviews of whom, helped the researcher to throw a light on the subject of FIR in India. The title of the book, "Reformation of Indian Judicial system" which is written by Sir Alexander P.J., provides satisfactorily analysis on the challenges faced by Judiciary while coping up with the Police department. Book, "Administration of justice in India" by Mann T.K., provided the ways to overcome these challenges which led to a state of confusion among Police and Judiciary. Book, "Police, Politics and Citizens rights" by Malviya P.D., has further led to explain the challenges and problems which are usually being faced by Police department while lodging any F.I.R. as well.

Research Methodology-

The research methodology adopted is both doctrinal & empirical in nature. In order to collect data, different tools & techniques are to be adopted. For eg...In case of collecting data for doctrinal research, the researcher would rely on primary sources such as articles, journals etc...as well as secondary sources such as books,magazines etc., and in order to collect data for empirical study the researcher will rely on surveys, interviews etc.

Research Gap-

After going through various literature available on the said topic it was found by the researcher that though the concept of F.I.R. has been touched by authors., however, the material available is either explaining the concept of F.I.R. that what it is, by providing an insight to the legality question. Researcher in order to overcome this ambiguity and also to make not only the comparison between various states with new amended legislation of 2013 and 2018, but also to critically analyse the impact of latest amendment sought to take up the said topic for research purpose. Thus, the present research has been taken up to answer the problems being faced by layman to lodge F.I.R, the problems being faced by Police and Judiciary[9]to tackle the subject as well.

Results & Suggestions-

FIR can be used to contradict an informant witness u/s 145 of Indian Evidence Act.FIR can be used by the defence to impeach the credit of the maker under sec. 155(3) of the Indian Evidence Act.A non-confessional FIR given by an accused can be used as an admission against him u/s 21 of Evidence Act of 1872. FIR can be used as a dying declaration as substantive evidence if it relates to the cause or occasion or circumstances and facts which resulted in the informant's death. within the meaning of section 32(1) of the Evidence Act. If the accused himself lodges the FIR, it cannot be used for corroboration or contradiction because the accused cannot be a prosecution witness, and he would very rarely offer himself to be a defence witness u/s 315 of the Code of Criminal procedure. In Raghbir Singh v. The State of Haryana[10], It was held that going to the hospital due to the condition of the victim for saving his life instead of going to the police station first was a reasonable and valid explanation for the delay in filing F.I.R. The object of early filing of F.I.R. to the police as soon as possible, in respect of the commission of the offence is to obtain and receive fresh information regarding the circumstances and facts which tend to result in the commission of the offence. The FIR shall have better corroborative value if it is recorded and taken before the informant's memory fades and before he starts to forget the facts. Thus, if there is a delay in lodging FIR and the delay is unreasonable and unexplained, it is likely to create scope for suspicion or introduction of a concocted story by the prosecution. It is the duty of the prosecution to explain the delay in lodging FIR. If satisfactorily explained, it does not lose its evidentiary value. However, mere delay in lodging FIR is not fatal to the prosecution case. In Harpal Singh v. State of Himachal Pradesh[11], It was held that 'delay of 10 days in lodging the first information report stands reasonably explained when the prosecution stated that as the honour of the family was involved, the members needed time to decide whether the matter should be taken to the court or not. In cases of rape and other sexual offences, the case is not only related to the victim but also with the family of the victim. Many times due to shame and honour they do not contact the police immediately. Therefore, the courts have consistently ruled that delay in a case of sexual assault cannot be equated with the case involving other offences.

Conclusive Proofs-

Lastly, the question arises that confessional statements can be utilised as FIR or not. If the FIR is a confessional one, it can be admissible. A confession is received in evidence on the presumption that no person will voluntarily make a statement which is against his or her interest, unless it is true. In case where there is confession made by the accused, the court decides to accept it by two factorsi.e. on the basis that whether the confession is voluntary and other is that whether the confession is true and trustworthy.

References-

BOOKS-

1. S.N. Mishra, "Indian Penal Code", Central Law Publications, TwentySecondedn., as per criminal law amendment 2018.

2. S.N. Mishra, "The Code of Criminal Procedure", Central Law Publications, Twenty-Second edn., as per criminal amendment 2018.

3. Kaleeswaram Raj, "Rethinking Judicial Reforms", Universal Law Publications

DICTIONARY-

1. Black's Law Dictionary, 8th edn., 1253.

REPORTS AND NEWSPAPER ARTICLES-

1. *The Hindu, October 22, 2013.*
2. *The Hindu, November 17, 2021.*
3. *The Tribune, May 5, 2022.*
4. *The Indian Express, June 1, 2022*

[1] Karl Olivecrona, "Appropriation in the State of Nature: Lock on the Origin of Property" in John Lock (1632-1704) Great

Western Political Thinkers, edited by Subrata Mukharjee and SushilaRamaswami, 409 (Deep and Deep Publication, New Delhi, 1994.

[2]Govt. of India, “Report of the committee on Reforms of Criminal Justice System” (Ministry of Home affairs, 2003).

[3]Bareact, The code of criminal procedure, 1973, Shree ram Law Publishers, Chd, 2023.

[4]Poongkhulali B, “All you must know about the FIR” The Hindu, October 22, 2013.

[5] Available at, First Information Report (FIR) under CrPC - Law Times Journal, visited on, (02,06,2022).

[6]Available at, Police Definition & Meaning - Merriam-Webster, visited on (06,06,2022).

[7]Poongkhulali B, “All you must know about the FIR” The Hindu, October 22, 2013

[8]Bareact, Indian Evidence Act(1872), Shree Ram Law House, Chd, 2023.

[9] S.S. Negi (Legal Correspondent), “FIR registeration must: SC” The Tribune ,New Delhi, July 24, 2022.

[10]Raghbir Singh Vs. State of Haryana 1980 SCR (3) 277.

[11]Harpal Singh Vs. State of HP AIR 1981 SC 361.

CHAPTER XIII

RIGHT TO HEALTH AND HEALTH CARE: AN INTERSECTION WITH RIGHT TO LIFE

{Author: Priyanka Bansal}

Individuals have the right to access the best possible mental as well as physical health, which includes healthcare services, medicine, and health information. This right is acknowledged by numerous international agreements on human rights, as well as the international standards and declarations relating to health. In India, the right to life is guaranteed by Article 21 of the Constitution, and the government is obligated under Part IV of the Indian Constitution to provide healthcare to the public[1]. The Apex Court and various High Courts have recognized the right to health and healthcare as a fundamental right and have imposed an obligation on the State itself to provide medical services. Health is a critical aspect of human development, which is necessary for a country's economic and social progress.

As humans, we prioritize the well-being of ourselves and our loved ones on a daily basis. Our health is of utmost importance to us, regardless of the factors as age, gender, socioeconomic status, or race. The right to have a good health is a fundamental human right, and is explicitly mentioned in multiple major international agreements. [2]

The ICESCR, or International Covenant on Economic, Social and Cultural Rights, regards the right to the "highest attainable standard of physical and mental health" as the most important. The World Health Organization defines the word 'health' in its introduction as "a state of complete physical, mental, and social well-being, not merely the absence of disease or infirmity." World Health Organisation also emphasizes that every human being, irrespective of race, religion, political belief, economic or social status, possesses the fundamental right to enjoy the finest possible standard of health.

Article 25 of the UDHR or Universal Declaration of Human Rights includes health as a part of the right to a decent living standard. Although the Indian Constitution does not explicitly identify the right to health as a fundamental right, Article 21 of the Indian Constitution guarantees the fundamental right to life and personal liberty. However, through various court judgments, the Indian Judiciary through a plenty of judgements has broadly interpreted Article to recognize the right to health as a fundamental right. Several provisions exist in the Indian Constitution concerning the right to health and healthcare. The Constitution mandates that the State ensures the formation and maintenance of conditions conducive to good health, as set out in Articles 38, [39 (e), (f)], 42, 47, and 48A in part IV. This article aims to provide valuable insights into the current state of right to health and healthcare under Article 21 of the Indian Constitution and its impact on individuals in India.[3] The research findings will inform policy and decision-making aimed at creating legislation on the right to health and healthcare, which is otherwise recognized under Article 21 of the Indian Constitution in India.

OBJECTIVES OF THE STUDY

1. To examine the current state of health and healthcare in India and its relationship with the right to health and healthcare envisaged in Article 21 of the Indian Constitution.
2. To identify the barriers and challenges to the implementation of the right to health and healthcare.
3. To assess the impact of these barriers and challenges on the health and healthcare access and outcomes of individuals in India.
4. To explore the role of the government, non-governmental organizations, and communities in promoting and protecting the right to health and healthcare under Article 21 of the Indian Constitution.

RESEARCH METHODOLOGY

The study will be conducted using a doctrinal research method that employs different approaches. Specifically, the investigation will rely on textbooks, published articles, court rulings, reports from committees and commissions, law journals, Indian legislation, foreign legislation, and newspaper articles.

CONCEPT AND IMPORTANCE OF THE RIGHT TO HEALTH AND HEALTHCARE

Article 21 of the Constitution states that no individual can be deprived of their personal liberty or life unless it is in accordance with the legal process.[4] The right to life entails more than mere physical existence, also to encompasses the right to live with respect and dignity. Hon'ble Supreme Court, in the landmark case *Consumer Education and Resource Centre vs Union of India*[5], ruled that the right to health and healthcare is a fundamental right under Article 21 as it is necessary for the life of the person to have meaning and purpose and to maintain their dignity. The "right to life" in Article 21 has a broad meaning, which also includes the right to a livelihood, a healthier standard of living, sanitary working conditions, and leisure time. The court stated that government, whether at the State or Union level, or a private or public industry, is required to take the necessary actions to promote the strength, health. In the case of *Bandhua Mukti Morcha vs Union of India*[6], the Hon'ble Supreme Court established that the right to a dignified life, which is protected by Article 21, is based on the Part IV of Indian Constitution that is directive principles of state policy and comprises the right to health. This was the first instance where the apex court recognized that humane working conditions are necessary for the fulfilment of the right to life. The court mandated that workers should have access to medical care, clean water, and sanitation facilities in order to live with dignity. The issue of whether the government's provision of medical services is sufficient was addressed in another landmark case of *Paschim Banga Khet Mazdoor Samiti vs State of Bengal*[7]. The apex court was asked to determine whether the lack of services in government health centres amounted to a violation of Article 21and the Hon'ble supreme court ruled that Article 21 places a responsibility on State to protect the right to life for every individual, and that the protection of human life is of utmost importance. It is the duty of government hospitals and their medical staff to provide medical assistance to preserve human life, and failure to do so violates the individual's right to life envisaged in Article 21 of the Indian Constitution. The apex court has held that the primary health care centres must be prepared to handle all the medical emergencies, and lack of pecuniary resources cannot be used as an excuse for the state to avoid its constitutional obligation. In another case of *State of Punjab and Others vs Mohinder Singh Chawla*[8], it was established that the right to health is a fundamental aspect of the right to life, and the government has a constitutional responsibility to provide health facilities. Despite government efforts, there are still challenges to be addressed, such as healthcare shortages, inadequate infrastructure and resources, and healthcare costs. The government should continue implementing policies to promote Universal Health Coverage and ensure all citizens have access to quality healthcare services without financial barriers. Access to healthcare remains limited in many countries, especially developing countries, despite the protection and recognition of the right to health and healthcare under international law. To address this issue, it is pertinent to understand the relationship between the right to health, healthcare, and life, and identify the factors that influence the promotion and protection of these rights. This study aims to contribute to this understanding by examining the extent to which the right to health and healthcare is being protected and the factors that affect this protection.

INTERNATIONAL SCENARIO

The UDHR or Universal Declaration of Human Rights, created in 1948 by the United Nations, includes Article 25 which guarantees every human being the right to have a satisfactory standard of living, including access to necessities such as food, housing, clothing, social services and medical care. Additionally, all individuals have the right to be protected during periods of unemployment, illness, widowhood, disability, old age, or other situations outside of their control. Special attention and assistance are to be provided for children and parenthood.[9] India, a founding member of the United Nations, has sanctioned various international conventions aimed at defending the healthcare rights of individuals. The World Health Organization has advocated for essential health services and procedures to achieve universal health coverage by the year 2000. However, the right to health cannot be achieved in isolation, as it is interconnected with the right to education, employment, food security, and information. By expanding the right to health and healthcare, the rights of Indian citizens will become more complete as intended by the framers of the Indian Constitution.[10] The focus on healthcare has increased due to rising morbidity and mortality rates in India, with non- communicable and communicable diseases on the rise. Infectious diseases remain a public health concern, and high maternal and child mortality rates persist. The right to health is known to be a fundamental human right in numerous international treaties, including the ICESCR or International Covenant on Economic, Social, and Cultural Rights and the Convention on the Rights of the Children. The former recognizes the right to health as an integral part of the right to a satisfactory standard of living, while the latter recognizes the right to health as a fundamental right for all children.

JUDICIAL RESPONSE

The fulfilment of the right to the highest achievable standard of health and its underlying determinants is a fundamental right of every individual residing within India. This includes the realisation of the right to free, accessible, and quality healthcare, access to the factors of health such as food, water, housing, sanitation, and a clean environment, access to information and education regarding health, and regulation of the determinants of health. In the famous case of *Francis Coralie Mullin v. Administrator, Union Territory of Delhi*[11], the Hon'ble Supreme Court of India held that Article 21 of the Constitution mandates the provision of necessities required for living with human dignity. The State is barred from discriminating among individuals under Articles 14, 15, 16 and 17, including on the grounds of race, religion, sex, caste, or place of birth. The State is also allowed to enact special measures for the upliftment of marginalised individuals and groups such as Dalit, Adivasi, indigenous, transgender, gender diverse individuals, and women and children. Human trafficking and forced labour are prohibited under Article 23, and the employment of children in any hazardous occupation is prohibited under Article 24[12]. The DPSP or Directive Principles of State Policy urge the State to minimise inequalities, secure a just social order, strive to secure a sufficient means of living, distribute the control and ownership of resources to serve the common good, ensure equal pay for equal work, also secure the health and strength of all workers, protect children from abandonment and abuse, and promote the overall development of children and adolescents.[13] Every individual should have equal opportunity for a fair trial and redressal of their rights violations under Article 39-A. Article 41 urges the State to secure the right to work, and public aid in case of unemployment, old age, disability and sickness.[14] Under Article 42, the State is obligated to ensure the humane caring working conditions that include maternity relief. Under Article 45, providing care to infants and children is a Directive Principle, and Article 47 encourages the State to improve public health by increasing nutrition and living standards. Article 48A calls on the State to safeguard the environment. The Hon'ble Supreme Court of India has established the right to health in numerous judgments[15]. In *C.E.S.C. Limited v. Subhash Chandra Bose*[16], the apex court defined the right to health as the attainment of complete physical, social, and intellectual well-being, instead of just the absence of illness. In *State of Punjab v. Ram Lubhaya Bagga* and *Devika Biswas v. Union of India*[17], the Court recognized the right to health under Article 21, which requires the State to provide healthcare services equivalent to those available in other hospitals. In the case of *Paschim Banga Khet Mazdoor Samity v. State of West Bengal*, emergency care was deemed central to the right to health. *Navtej Singh Johar v. Union of India*[18]confirmed the right of individuals to control their health and body and access healthcare services that offer equal opportunities for the descent level of health. The State has a responsibility to ensure the right to health and healthcare and the underlying factors of health for all individuals within its territory, as stipulated by international conventions such as the UDHR or Universal Declaration of Human Rights, the ICESCR or International Covenant on Economic, Social and Cultural Rights, the International Covenant on Civil and Political Rights, the Convention on the Rights of the Child, the Convention on the Elimination of all Forms of Discrimination against Women, the UN Convention on Rights of Persons with Disabilities, the Declaration of Alma-Ata, and the Programme for Action of International Conference on Population and Development, and the International Health Regulations. The State cannot shirk its duty to fulfil this right due to financial constraints. During the COVID-19 pandemic, the Hon'ble Supreme Court of India affirmed that the right to health includes the right to affordable treatment under Article 21 and urged the Central Government to enhance protections for healthcare workers.

CONCLUSION

The courts have recognized the right to health and healthcare as a fundamental right protected under the right to life under Article 21 of the Indian Constitution. The Supreme Court has interpreted this right under the Directive Principles of State Policy in the Constitution of India, specifically within the context of the State's responsibility to provide for and safeguard the health of its citizens. The Supreme Court has also determined that the right to health is an essential element of the right to life, and therefore a fundamental right enshrined in the Indian Constitution.[19]

There is a growing debate over whether an amendment to the Constitution is necessary to explicitly establish the right to health and healthcare as a fundamental right and hold the State accountable for any violations. This article aims to contribute to this discourse by providing a comprehensive understanding of the relationship between the right to health, the right to life, and the legislative and judicial frameworks in India and internationally. Policymakers, lawyers, and healthcare professionals can utilize the findings of this study to advocate for the realization of these fundamental rights in India.

REFRENCES

1. The Constitution of India (Article 21) - Right to Life and Personal Liberty
2. The Right to Health and Healthcare Bill, 2021
3. The Medical Termination of Pregnancy (Amendment) Act, 2021
4. The Mental Healthcare Act 2017
5. The Clinical Establishments (Registration and Regulation) Act, 2010
6. The Indian Medical Council (Professional Conduct, Etiquette and Ethics) Regulations, 2002
7. The Persons with Disabilities (Equal Opportunities, Protection of Rights and Full Participation) Act, 1995
8. The Medical Termination of Pregnancy Act, 1971
9. The PNDT (Pre-Conception and Pre-Natal Diagnostic Techniques) Act1994

WEBLIOGRAPHY

1. www.penacclaims.com.
2. https://www.un.org
3. https://www.ncbi.nlm.nih.gov
4. https://indiankanoon.org

CHAPTER XIV

TRANSGENDER PERSONS (PROTECTION OF RIGHTS) ACT: AN OVERVIEW {Author: Ravneet Kaur}

Who are Transgender?

Transgender is an umbrella term for people whose gender identity or expression differs from the sex assigned to them at birth. A transgender person, for example, may identify as a woman despite being born with male genitalia. Transgender people are those whose gender identity, gender expression, or behaviours differ from those normally associated with their assigned gender. Gender identity is a person's internal sense of being male, female, or something else. Gender expression is the way a person communicates their gender identity to others through their behaviour, clothing, hairstyle, voice, or physical characteristics. "**Trans**" is an abbreviation for "**transgender**". Transgender is a good term in general, but not everyone who is gender nonconforming in appearance or behaviour can be labelled as transgender. Transgender people's treatment is changing all the time, especially as people become more aware, knowledgeable, and open about transgender people and their experiences.

It includes trans-person with intersex variations, gender-queer and person having such socio-cultural identities as **kinnar, hijra, aaravani** and **jogta.**

Transgender in India:

In India, gender differences go back to ancient times, maybe even prehistoric times. **Hijras, Eunuchs, Kothis, Aravanis, Jogappas, Shiv-Shakthis,** etc. are members of the TG community. Over 4000 years of history are known about the hijra community in India. The **Hijras** belonged to the eunuch culture that was common in India and the Middle East, where **Eunuchs** served as protectors, counsellors, and entertainers. The **Ramayana** and **Mahabharata**, two classical works of Hindu mythology, are the sources of the **hijra**.

The hijra was also important in the Islamic world's courts, particularly in the Ottoman and Mughal Empires of medieval Society. Hijra/transgender people have historically played an important role, but the situation changed significantly with the arrival of colonial rule in the 18th century. The Criminal Tribes Act of 1871, which was passed when the Hijra community was under British control, declared the entire group to be essentially addicts and criminals who routinely committed crimes without posting bail. The law was overturned in 1949 after India gained independence, but prejudice against the transgender community still exists.

The transgender community, also known as Hijras in this country, is a subset of Indian citizens who are frequently subject to ridicule and even fear due to superstition, according to a 2014 ruling from the Supreme Court. Additionally, everyone, including transgender people, transgender people, and hijras, should have the freedom to choose how they want to express their gender. They ought to have had the freedom to identify as a third gender and the ability to freely express that. Thus, third gender is the term used today to refer to transgender people in India. All over India, there are hijras. Despite collecting data for many years, the Indian Census has never accepted the third gender, or transgender people. However, information was gathered in 2011 about transgender people's employment, education, and caste. The **2011 census** estimates that there are **4.88 lakh** transgender people living in India.

Hijra are distinctive due to their active social organisation in both tradition and ritual. They support themselves by engaging in prostitution or carrying out religious ceremonies like rituals. It is a family gathering with singing, dancing, and music at the baby's home. It should be noted that not everyone agrees with this ritual, though. The **Transgender (Protecting Rights) Bill 2016** was approved by the **Union Cabinet** for inclusion in Parliament and is anticipated to give the community social, educational, and economic empowerment transgender. This action could represent a chance for a community that has endured so much hatred and discrimination to live in dignity and equality.

In spite of this seemingly accepted role in Indian culture, transgender people experience severe discrimination and harassment in the country today, as well as unfair treatment. In many contexts, including family members, academic facilities, workplaces, healthcare facilities, and public spaces, victims can experience verbal, physical, and sexual abuse as well as false arrests, refusal to share ancestors' goods and services, exclusion from admission to educational institutions, and verbal, physical, and sexual abuse themselves. Parents, siblings, friends, neighbours, others in their community, school and university administrators, employers, landlords, healthcare professionals, police officers, and many other people have been known to violently or discriminatorily treat transgender people because of their appearance, feminine behaviour, or transgender status as well as their actual or imagined affiliation with commercial sex, HIV status, dress code, or other factors.

Difficulties Faced by Transgender Community:

There are many difficulties faced by transgender people in India. In addition to denying TG individuals equal access to essential social services like employment, healthcare, education, and housing, this discrimination also excludes them from society and adds them to the list of vulnerable groups at risk of social exclusion.

- **Inequality in the workplace and in the education system-**

The majority of the residents of this community are illiterate or uneducated, which limits their ability to participate in a society that values education. Only 46% of the 4.9 million transgender people in the United States can read and write, which is a very low percentage compared to the general population's literacy rate of 74%. They fall under the definition of "disadvantaged group" as defined by the Right to Education Act. In other words, 25% of them are set aside for groups who are economically disadvantaged. Poverty, social exclusion from family and friends, and psychological issues can all contribute to low levels of education. Even those who struggle to obtain an education and those who are unable to find employment will not be treated equally in the workplace if education is not available.

- **Victims of hate crimes and a lack of legal protection-**

Transgender people are less protected by law than other groups, making them more likely to become victims of crimes they did not commit. Many police departments are insensitive to these communities and will not even register any complaints they receive. They are being silenced by the police, showing how ineffective we are as citizens.

- **Homelessness and social exclusion-**

The transgender community has been neglected because there aren't enough educational and employment opportunities, and they're viewed as a lower class by society. This exclusion has such a negative impact on their self-esteem and self-confidence that they are forced into positions they don't want.

They run away from home because of abusive relationships and lose shelter and a place to call home, or they are expelled from their own homes because they are unaccepted by their own families.

- **Transphobia and psychological stress management-**

In comparison to heterosexual people, the transgender community faces much harassment, discrimination, and intolerance from society. Few people develop transphobia as a result of moral, religious, or social beliefs that lead to aggression, denial, or workplace harassment. For all of the aforementioned reasons, communities face numerous mental health issues and may make negative decisions such as self-harm and suicidal thoughts. Because of society, they are lonely. They are afraid and anxious.

- **Legal Problems-**

    - Section 377 makes adult consensual homosexual relationships in private illegal.
    - Lack of awareness of marriage
    - Violation of human and civil rights (especially for transgender)

In order to participate in culture, community, and movement, transgender people must raise awareness. The Equal Protection Clause of the Constitution may be broken when discrimination and harassment are aimed at transgender people and gender-converted students, according to federal law.

- **Problem with Identity-**

In 1994, transgender people won the right to vote, but the job of issuing them voter cards was replaced by issues of men versus women card was declined.

Transgender Person Protection (Rights Act) 2019:

In India, there are 4.9 lakh transgender people overall, according to the 2011 Census. The highest levels of social abuse and neglect are experienced by them. They frequently have their rights violated. They are viewed as criminals and social outcasts. As a result, the government passed the **Transgender Persons (Protection of Rights) Bill 2019** to ensure their socioeconomic justice. Under this law, a transgender person is described as a person whose gender does not correspond to the sex assigned to them at birth and includes a transgender male or a transgender female, a person with other transgender, a transgender person and a person with such social attitudes, cultural position, identities like **Kinner, hijra, aravani** and **jogta.**

It was launched on **19th July 2019** by **Mr. Thawardand Gehlot,** Minister for Social Justice and Empowerment. The law received his presidential approval on **December 5, 2019**, and the Transgender Persons (Protection of Rights) Act has been in effect since **January 10, 2020.**

There have been various petitions submitted contesting the lawfulness of the act. The **Transgender (Rights Protection) Code 2020** was introduced on **September 25, 2020**, by the Department, which had previously published the draft regulations in April 2020.

AIM of the Transgender Bill 2019:

- Reducing the social stigma connected to transgender people.
- Avoiding discrimination and abuse against transgender people.
- Assure transgender people's fundamental and basic rights.
- Beginning to integrate them into society's mainstream.

Highlights of the Act:

1. The **bill defines a transgender person** as someone whose gender does not match the gender they were assigned at birth. This includes trans men and trans women, individuals with intersex variations, genderqueer, and individuals with sociocultural identities such as kinahs and hijras ; defined as a person born with major sexual, genital, chromosomal, or hormonal deviations from the norm.
2. The **bill prohibits discrimination** against transgender people, including exclusion from services and abuse in the areas of:

(i) Employment
(ii) Education.
(iii) Medical services;
(iv) Use of any publically accessible products, services, or opportunities;

(v) The Right to Free Movement.

(vi) Possibilities to hold public or private office;

(vii) The right to live on, rent, or otherwise occupy property.

(viii) Having access to public or private facilities that treat or accommodate transgender people;

1. All transgender people have the **right to stay** and be included in the family. If a close relative is unable to care for a transgender person, the person may be placed in a rehabilitation center by order of the court of competent jurisdiction.
2. No public or private organization has the right to discriminate against transgender people in hiring, advancement, or other **employment-related decisions**. Every establishment must appoint a representative to handle complaints related to the Act as the complaint officer.
3. A **certificate of identity** with the gender category "transgender" may be requested from the District Magistrate by a transgender person. Only if the person has surgery to change their gender, either as a man or a female, is a new certificate possible.
4. According to the bill, responsible governments will take action to guarantee transgender people's full inclusion and involvement in society. Additionally, it should implement plans for their rescue and rehabilitation, **professional development**, and independence, as well as **develop programs** to help transgender persons and promote their involvement in cultural events.
5. The following **offences and penalties** are recognized by the Transgender Persons Act, and the sentence ranges from six months to two years in jail and a fine:

(i) forcing transgender people to engage in forced or bonded labour,

(ii) forcing transgender people to engage in forced or contracted labour,

(iii) denying them access to public spaces,

(iv) evicting them from their homes or villages,

(v) abusing them physically, sexually, verbally, emotionally, or financially.

The **National Council for Transgender (NCT)** was established by the Center and is presided over by the Union Social Justice Minister. It is made up of representatives from 10 central departments, five states or union territories, and five individuals who identify as transgender.

There are five primary duties of the National Council for Transgender (NCT):

(i) Analyzing and assessing the results of policies and initiatives aimed at attaining equality and full inclusion for transgender people.

(ii) Resolving transgender people's complaints.

(iii) Assisting the central government in creating transgender-related policies, programmes, regulations, and projects.

(iv) Examining and coordinating the work of all departments.

(v) Completing any additional tasks that the Center specifies.

National Legal Services Authority (NALSA) Vs Union of India (AIR 2014 SC)

According to the Court, discrimination on the basis of "sex" is expressly forbidden by Articles 15 and 16. Here, the term "sex" covers gender (depending on one's opinion of oneself) and biological features (such as chromosomes, genitalia, and secondary sexual characteristics).

The Court also interpreted Section 21 of the Constitution to include diversity in self-expression, which allows a person to lead a decent life. The fundamental right to dignity based on gender identity is also covered by article 21. It should be noted that the right to equality (article 14) and freedom [delete] of section 19(1)(a)) open to transgender people. The Court found that under sections 14, 15, 16, 19(1)(a) and 21 of the Constitution, transgender people enjoy basic rights.

The Court also highlighted the need for public education campaigns to overcome discrimination against the transgender community. Additionally, it instructed both the Central and State

Governments to include clauses in all legal documents recognising third gender individuals as members of the socially and educationally needy class who are entitled to reservations in learning institutions and public jobs.

It was a significant decision for being the first to take the non-binary gender identity seriously and protect the basic rights of transgender people in India.

Hina Haneefa Vs State of Kerala (WP Civil 23404/2020)

A transgender woman who had sex reassignment surgery and obtained a transgender identity card indicating her gender identify as a woman is the petitioner. Due to the applicant's transgender identity, the National Cavalry Corps rejected her application for membership in the Women's Team. In accordance with the Transgender Act, which prohibits discrimination against transgender people, the court decided that the petitioner should be permitted to enter the Women's Division

Analysis of the Act:

1. The Transgender Act's definition of transgender is inaccurate since there is a distinction between a transgender people who has an identity other than the one they were given at birth and someone who has "intersex variants," or sex based on biological traits.
2. The silent law on transgender reserves tries to reserve transgender individuals as a socially and educationally backward class, contradicting a Supreme Court judgement in the 2014 NALSA case.
3. The consequences for crimes against transgender people are only up to two years in prison and a fine, which is insufficient for other offences such as sexual abuse, rape, and violent assault.
4. To accept their identity, the Transgender Persons Act 2019 requires the person to seek for a transgender certificate, which certifies their gender as transgender. It further states that if a person receives sex determination surgery, a certificate of amendment must be issued by a District Judge, who has the

ability to evaluate the validity of the application and whether or not evidence of sex determination surgery is included. The Transgender Bill 2020 restrictions make obtaining a transgender certificate complex and frustrating.

5. The Transgender Bill 2020 expands children' residency rights by mandating transgender people under the age of 18 to live with their birth family. This can represent a risk to transgender people because the family is frequently a source of abuse against the transgender community. The bill also criminalizes begging, but it makes no provisions for employment or education reservations.

INTIATIVE BY GOVERNMENT TAKEN FOR TRANSGENDER PERSONS

1. **Transgender Persons (Protection of Rights) Rules, 2020-**

- The rules were introduced under the Transgender Persons (Protection of Rights) Act 2019.
- The regulations aim to recognize the identity of transgender people and forbid discrimination in the areas of healthcare, education, employment, property ownership or disposal, access to and use of public services and benefits, and holding public or private office.

2. **Garima Greh-**

- The Ministry of Social Justice and Empowerment officially opened Garima Greh, a refuge home for transgender people, in November 2020.
- The "transgender shelter" programme offers services like housing, food, clothing, recreation, opportunities for skill development, yoga, fitness, library facilities, legal assistance, transgender and surgical counselling methods, capacity building for organisations that support transgender people, employment,

etc.

- A minimum of 25 transgender people will receive rehabilitation under the programme in each of the homes chosen by the Ministry.
- To establish the 13 Shelter Homes, 10 cities have been chosen.

3. **Indian Prisoner Recognition-**

- In January 2022, the Ministry of Home Affairs issued a recommendation to the heads of prisons in the states and territories to preserve the privacy and dignity of third-gender convicts.
- In 2020, there were 70 transgender prisoners in jails across the country, according to the National Crime Records Bureau.
- The Prisons Act 1894 of India does not recognise sexual minorities based on Sexual Orientation and Gender Identity (SOGI) as a separate class of convicts.

4. **National Portal for Transgender Persons-**

- In January 2022, the Department of Home Affairs issued a notice to state/UT prison directors to ensure the privacy and dignity of third-sex inmates.

  - This will help them track the status of their application, denials, complaint resolution, and more, which will ensure transparency in the process.

- It was launched in accordance with the 2020 Transgender Persons (Protection of Rights) Rules.

5. **Transgender Inclusive Policies –**

- Legal systems and law enforcement must be empowered and responsive to the transgender community's concerns.
- A comprehensive approach to transgender people must be planned and approved by government and society.

CONCLUSION-

Living in a community that still battles to find its identity in the modern, digital age. Anyone who does not identify with the gender given to them at birth is considered transgender. For many years now, they have experienced rejection and discrimination. They do not have the same rights, identities, or dignity as other people. A better society for transgender people is something we are working toward slowly but surely. The law that was passed, however, is less theoretical than it is practical.

The Transgender Persons (Protection of Rights) Act 2019 has seen some progress, but there is still plenty of room for change. India has adopted some elements of its constitution from several other countries. Similarly, when analyzing the position of transgender people around the world, researchers came across a range of arrangements that could be integrated and adapted in India as well. These include specific laws prohibiting discrimination in various areas of life, legal recognition of same-sex marriage, and medical due process.

About The Authors

- Vipul R. R. Malhotra:

Author is a Research Scholar at student at Rajiv Gandhi National University of Law, Patiala, Punjab

- Ravneet Kaur

Author is working as Assistant at Jeevan Institute, Patiala.

- Manju Kumari

Author is a practising Advocate at Punjab and Haryana High Court, Chandigarh

- Alisha Gupta

Author is a practising Advocate at Punjab and Haryana High Court, Chandigarh

- Amardeep Singh

Author is an Advocate

- Mehak Dalla

Author is an Advocate

- Priyanka

Author is an Associate Professor

- Arpandeep Kaur

Author is an Advocate

- Heena

Author is an Advocate

- Dr. Gurpreet Kaur

Author is Professor at Gurukashi University.

- Ginni Singla

Author is LL.M. student at Gurukashi University.

- Babanpreet Kaur

Author is a practising Advocate at Punjab and Haryana High Court, Chandigarh

- Dhruv Gupta

Author is an Advocate

- Navneet Bhathal

Author is an Advocate

- Navjot Kaur

Author is an Advocate

Printed by Libri Plureos GmbH in Hamburg,
Germany